# *The*
# *Last Boat Out*

## *Memoirs of a Triumphant Vietnamese-American Family*

*by*

Truong-Nhu Dinh

*and*

Tran Thi Truong Nga

Translated by Truong-Nhu Kenny
and Ton-Nu Phuong-Thao

GASLight Publishing
512-528-1727
PO Box 1025
Leander, TX 78646
info@gaslightpublishing.com

E-BOOK
ISBN 13 e-book: 978-09754796-7-4
ISBN 10 e-book: 09754796-7-9

PAPERBACK
ISBN 13 paperback: 978-09754796-6-7
ISBN 10 paperback: 09754796-6-0

Library of Congress Control Number: 2006922838

The events in these memoirs are true and described accurately to the best of
the authors' recollections and research. Some names have been abbreviated
to protect privacy.

# Quotes from Family and Friends

When we initially set foot in the States…, I … did not know …we actually were homeless, broke, and without a certain future… our parents' goal was that each of the six children would graduate from universities… The 21 years of hardship and struggles paid off in a big way. … My siblings and I owe so much to (our) role-model parents.
— Truong-Nhu Ngoc (daughter)

I was born in the right family, and I would like to keep my family tradition, the Truong-Nhu tradition, alive.
— Truong-Nhu Kenny (son)

Bless you, Truong family, for I have been blessed to be a part of your lives and to have the opportunity to learn so much from you.
— Your grateful son, Duc (son-in-law Douglas Starr)

Thank you for your life's story. We will all cherish it. McKenzie, Kennedi, Doug, and I love you very much. You have given me a cherished childhood, and now you are giving your grandchildren cherished memories.
— With all my heart, LOVE, Thuy Truong Starr (daughter)

As we all grow older and wiser, I can only wish to be half the "parents" that my parents are. I hope that my wife and I have learned from them and teach future generations about what parents should really be.
— Truong-Nhu Dzung (son)

I feel like the luckiest person in the world … I'm glad I have grown from a "bratty" kid to a responsible adult, and I have my parents to thank.
— Anh Truong Gist (daughter)

I am so proud for what my parents have accomplished. They are truly an inspiration to me, and I hope I can make them just as proud of me as I am of them.
— Amy Truong Craig (daughter)

Nobody ever told me what exactly happened ... It wasn't until I read the first few chapters of my grandma's autobiography that I knew the whole, truthful story. It was a sad, haunting tale — one that made me admire my soft-spoken, cheerful grandparents even more.
— Ailien Phan (granddaughter)

I admire the Truong-Nhu for writing this book and sharing their true stories about this important subject. There are misunderstandings about the war; this book will educate everyone about the truth of the sacrifices that the Americans and the South Vietnamese endured. Without dramatic structures or novel manipulations, the book demonstrates the impact of the war on a civilian aspect.
— Mr. Ton-That Duong (former South Vietnamese officer)

The memoirs of Mr. and Mrs. Dinh Truong are golden documents for Americans to understand a successful newly immigrated family in America and also for future young Vietnamese American generations to learn how their pioneers immigrated to the United States.
— Mr. Truong-Nhu Lam (cousin)

We are proud of our relationship that has been established for the past 30 years and will continue into coming years. Again the Truong family and the Ngo family are ONE FAMILY. Our children know that, our friends know that, and we would like to keep that as a gift GOD gave to us forever.
— Mr. Ngo Lang (former South Vietnamese Navy Officer, Lt. J.G.)

# *D*edication

With respect and remembrance
to our fathers and mothers, who are deeply missed:

Sir Truong-Nhu Ngan (1900-1943)
Sir Tran Dinh Dai (1906-1968)
Mrs. Pham Thi Lang (1907-1981)
Mrs. Le Thi Nguyet (1913-1986)

With much love and hope to the
future Truong-Nhu generations.
Our children, who deserve nothing
but the best for being so wonderful:

Truong-Nhu Ngoc
Truong-Nhu Kenny
Truong-Nhu Thuy
Truong-Nhu Dzung
Truong-Nhu Phuong-Anh
Truong-Nhu Amy

Our children-in-law, who help make
a better future for the Truong-Nhu family:

Phan Canh Thanh
Ton-Nu Phuong-Thao
Douglas Starr
Tran Ha Vu-Thy
Bryan Gist
Rob Craig

Our grandchildren, who are the
hope and joy of their grandparents:

Phan Ailien
Phan Caitlin
Phan Ty
McKenzie Starr
Kennedi Starr
Emma Gist
Truong-Nhu Nicholas
Natalie Craig
And others in the future ...

*Authors,*
*Truong-Nhu Dinh & Tran Thi Truong Nga*

# Contents

# Preface

While one English proverb states, "Let bygones be bygones," the Chinese Vietnamese proverb states the opposite, *On co tri tan,* or "Review the past to predict the future." According to this Asian thinking, it is not a waste to review the past.

We are Asian at heart. We have written our memoirs to document the past, a historical past that is very hard to forget. There were times we were happy. There were times we were very sad. There were moments of heart-felt misery, but there were also moments of shining pride. The older we get and the closer we are to forgetting, the more important it is to us that our family learns about the past with all the ups and downs of our lives. These memoirs are intended to capture all the obstacles the Truong-Nhu family has experienced and overcome, especially during the Vietnam War.

We hope this book will help to answer some questions about civilian life in Vietnam and the part of the Truong-Nhu family in the big picture of Vietnamese history. We hope this book will help future generations understand about our ancestors. We are not rich, so we do not have a lot of property to share with our children, but we have our experiences and lessons to pass on. We hope our future generations will appreciate the past, keep the traditions, value education, and become good citizens of society. We hope the future generations understand that their existence takes meaning from the past. Without the past, no matter whether it is a sad or a happy one, there will be no existence of the present time or the future.

While the two authors have individual experiences, we share a common view about the war and the impact of war on Vietnamese civilian life. We both experienced the hardships of running from the communists. We both experienced the uncertainty of political chaos from the division of Vietnam in 1954 through the Tet Offensive in 1968, the Red Summer in 1972, and the run from the Vietcong in 1973 to the fall of Saigon in 1975.

We had different backgrounds in our childhoods and early lives, but we shared the hardship of starting over. Despite our different experiences, we both share the very foundation of what it takes to be happy in life. We appreciate the values of Vietnamese tradition and family, and we praise the value of education. We appreciate America, the land of opportunity. We appreciate where we came from and what life has to offer. The appreciation extends to our family, relatives, and friends, without whom we would not have had the motivation to tell our story.

This book was written based upon our memories of Vietnam, the war, and life in America for immigrants like us. The book was originally intended to capture the history of the Truong-Nhu family, but it touched the heart of a professional writer, who introduced it to a publisher. GASLight Publishing saw the value of the book for the general public because of its details associated with the Vietnam War and the Vietnamese people.

In some cases, real names have been shortened or changed to protect the privacy of individuals who prefer not to be publicly identified or to avoid misunderstanding of their views or actions.

We thank the publisher, especially Grace Anne Schaefer, for recognizing how the book can be delivered to a wider audience. We thank the editors, especially Lillie Ammann, for spending so much time in editing and working with us to make this a reality. We thank our beloved daughters and sons and daughters-in-law and sons-in-law, as well as relatives and friends who expressed their feelings upon reading the documents. Their feedback enriched the book with different views and interpretations.

*Truong-Nhu Dinh & Tran Thi Truong Nga*

# Dad: Leaving Vietnam

We could see the Anh Tuan ship anchored at the Khanh Hoi Port. To get inside the port to the ship, we had to pass through a long row of circle barbed wire. My brother-in-law H told us each person had to bend his body to pass through the barbed wire. After H and his daughter HP passed through the wire, he said he had to meet my sister Tran who was already on board, so he couldn't wait for us. He gave me directions to join him and his family once we had passed through the fence.

After he left, I pushed our two bags through, then I placed my hands in front while bending my body between the sharp wires. I wriggled through the fence and gave directions for my family, one by one, to do the same. I helped each of my five children from the port side while my mother-in-law and my wife Nga encouraged them from the other side.

Everyone else passed through the fence without any problem, but Nga couldn't bend half of her body because of the severe leg injury she'd received during the Tet Offensive. She had to lie down while I held the wires open so she could move forward. I could see her body scraping the ground, causing major scratches from her chest to her leg. It hurt me to see her struggling, but with all of our lives at risk, she had to succeed. We had only one chance to reach the ship — the pressure pushed us forward.

Though there were no regulation or check points inside the port, taking the kids across the temporary wooden bridge to the ship proved to be a huge challenge. The bridge was barely wide enough for a single person, and the water was fairly deep. I saw many people, including small children, elbowing each other to reach the Anh Tuan ship. We had to be very careful not to fall into the water in the middle of this chaos.

There was no one to help, as all were running for their own lives. People fought over good spots on board, and no one seemed to care about children or the elderly. After helping my mother-in-law across the bridge, I made several round trips to help the children on board. With my mother-in-law and the five children safely on the ship, I made one last trip to help Nga.

Since she didn't know how to swim, the swirling water beneath the creaky plank and the unpleasant squeak the bridge made with every movement intimidated and unnerved her. At the other end of the bridge, our children cried for their mother. They stood beside my mother-in-law, but their eyes watched every step Nga took. As we walked step by step across on the narrow bridge, I spoke words of encouragement.

"The children made it, and so can you. We have to make it across. If one of us falls, we might miss the ship's departure schedule. You're almost there; you're almost there ..."

We finally made it on board the Anh Tuan ship, all eight of us. Our children clapped their hands and ran to hug us.

We were among the last groups who managed to leave Vietnam on the Anh Tuan ship. All the good seats had been taken, so we had to sit in a corner, close to the balcony without cover. I couldn't find my sister Tran and her family on the large ship, but at least my immediate family was together. Nga was bleeding from scratches over most of her body, but otherwise, we were in good shape. I breathed a huge sigh of relief that we'd all made it safely on board.

But I wondered what had happened to my mother, and worries about her made my chest hurt. I felt so helpless — I had to focus on getting the family members I had with me to safety, but I didn't know if my mother had made it out of DaNang. Thoughts of her inflicted a physical pain in my stomach. Even though I didn't say a word about her, I wondered if she was safe or even still alive in this chaos.

As I sat there thankful that my mother was the only person I had to worry about, my mother-in-law stunned us and added another worry. She told us for the first time that Nga's two brothers had been following the Vietcong since 1954. They had left their good jobs at the Central Hospital to move to the North, because, my mother-in-law said, they had an illusion about communism and what they could do to change the world.

She said to Nga, "I don't know where your two older brothers, Anh Hai and Anh Ba, are, but I feel I must stay in Vietnam to have a chance to see them again. I haven't seen them for over twenty years."

Nga and all of us sat there in total surprise and shock. The brothers' involvement with the Vietcong had been a well-kept secret.

My mother-in-law continued, "I love all of you very much, and I always will. But I need to close an important chapter of my life, and I need to be here in Vietnam to do it. Nga, your sister Le and her family are still stuck in DaNang. I can't leave them, either. Vietnam is my home; I'm just too old to leave." She turned to me. "Dinh, will you please walk me back to the other side of the bridge?"

We didn't know what to say. Nga was devastated, and our son Phuc, who was seven at the time, took it the hardest. After the Tet Offensive, Phuc had become very close to his grandmother, who had risked her life to get medical treatment for him.

Nga opened a secret wallet hidden under her shirt to give my mother-in-law some money. "Please take care of yourself." We all cried, but we realized each of us had to make choices for our own lives. We knew the decision to stay in Vietnam was a very difficult choice for my mother-in-law, but we ran out of time to debate about her decision. So I nodded my head in answer to her request.

As I walked Nga's mother back across the narrow plank bridge, people looked at us in surprise. It just didn't make sense for someone to walk back to the war-torn land while everyone else was desperately trying to escape. It just didn't make sense for a grandmother to walk away from the children she loved who were crying for her. The pain felt like a vice squeezing my heart, and I knew it was even more painful for Nga.

I almost exploded with the pain thinking of the difficulty both our mothers were facing in taking care of themselves at their ages. While it was hard to contact my mother, it was even harder to let my mother-in-law go — it's never easy to say goodbye forever to someone you love so dearly.

And we were saying goodbye forever not only to our mothers and to our homeland, but to life as we had known it. Squeezing my mother-in-law's hand, I said goodbye and asked her to take care of herself. Turning, I ran back to the Anh Tuan ship with an emotion hard to describe.

Goodbye, Vietnam. Hello, New Life ... wherever that might be.

CHAPTER 1

# Dad: Who I Am

Eyewitness to decades of conflict in Vietnam, I was a South Vietnamese military officer who came to the United States when Saigon fell to the Vietcong.

I was born in Hue in the late 1930s. Like many other Vietnamese of the same generation, I had an uncertain life in Vietnam, if not a very turbulent one.

When we left our home for the United States in 1975, our family just ran for our lives. Years in America have taught me to be humble, because I understand I came here for a better life, with a hope to live peacefully, to build a good family foundation so my children would have a better education and opportunities.

It was a miracle I saw all of my children finish their college educations. I am grateful for what I have here in the United States, but I had struggles with the memories of our mothers and the relatives we left behind.

After being constantly on the run from communists because of many sad historical events that affected our family in depth, I value strong family roots and the integrity of the South Vietnamese Government. During the Vietnam War, I saw images of major disruptions, such as the sight of communist forces in Hue during the Tet Offensive or their shooting down South Vietnamese officials and civilians. My older brother's death was an example.

I hope that the memoirs I share with you will help you understand our family history as well as learn more about Vietnamese history. I hope you can connect the past to maintain a better future for yourself and your loved ones.

## CHAPTER 2

# Mom: Who I Am

I am a traditional Vietnamese woman — a daughter, a daughter-in-law, a mother, and a grandmother. Born in Hue in the 1940's, I have experienced the cultures of both the East and the West; been through the Vietnam War with tears and sorrows, smiles and happiness; struggled through parts of my life; earned a living to help raise our children; and felt pride when our children grew up and graduated from American colleges.

I appreciate where I came from. I believe that Buddha blesses us during both up and down times of life. I believe in the values of Vietnamese Americans and in good family traditions. I believe in the freedom and generosity of America. I am proud to be a Vietnamese American ... and as many other Americans, I have stories to tell.

I hope these stories, my memories from the Tet Offensive in 1968 to the present of 2005, will help my children and their generation realize that all the things they have now — food to eat, educations, careers, families, friends, and freedom — are not to be taken for granted.

I hope that after reading these memoirs, my family will

keep the stories alive and pass them on to the next generation. Do not to be sad, but be proud and understand about the past — a very distinguished past not everyone has experienced. I hope you, the reader, will cherish your own heritage as well as mine and preserve it for future generations.

CHAPTER 3

# Dad: Vietnam History and Where I Came From

*"War is an ugly thing, but not the ugliest of things: the decayed and degraded state of moral and patriotic feeling which thinks nothing is <u>worth</u> a war, is worse. ... A man who has nothing which he is willing to fight for, nothing which he cares more about than he does about his personal safety, is a miserable creature who has no chance of being free, unless made and kept so by the exertions of better men than himself."*
                                                    *—John Stuart Mill*

Yes, war is an ugly thing, but perhaps my brothers had many reasons to go to war, not because they had chosen to, but because they were forced to. We had no other choices when our country was invaded and when innocent family members were killed. We did not take lives for granted. There was an expensive price for freedom. A peaceful life was not easy for us.

I was born in the year World War II began when Japanese forces occupied Vietnam. I was born at a time when the communists' propaganda was expanding, when communists were undercover as Viet Minh, or "the league for the independence of Vietnam." I was born at a time when the Viet Minh organization, led by Ho Chi Minh, became popular and attractive to many Vietnamese nationalists. Perhaps this explained why Nga's brothers were among the nationalists who joined the Viet Minh — perhaps they were moved by the idealism of a united Vietnam, independent from the rules and domination of foreigners such as the Japanese and French. I was born in a time when the Viet Minh were helped by both America and China, and, certainly, I was too young to contribute a sound political argument.

I was too young to understand why the Empire of Japan attacked the American military forces on Oahu in Hawaii and created a heart-rending tragedy at Pearl Harbor. When World War II ended in 1945, Vietnam was in a confused state, in the transformation of the Royalty regime to a yet-undefined Westernized culture. I was too young to comprehend all the changes. My childhood was immersed in Vietnamese tradition and custom, in the comfortable and secure world created by my mother.

I was taught to respect the *Quan, Su, Phu* morality, which translates to "King, Teacher, and Father," always listed in that order. Several generations of my family had served the Nguyen regime, and my brothers and I were taught to be very patriotic and modest. When I grew up, the King no longer ruled Vietnam and most of my teachers were influenced by French colonial-style education. After my father passed away, I counted on my mother to provide me with daily guidance and support.

I grew up in Hue, seat of the Kingdom of Vietnam traditions and royal domination. For more than a thousand years,

Hue had been through many historical events. People from Hue had a unique character that many people from the South envied. My mother was proud of the fact we were from Hue, and she taught that pride to me and my siblings. My mother told me Truong-Nhu was one of the most famous family surnames in Hue's history, and I was lucky to be born into the Truong-Nhu family, with the privilege to advance with higher education. I was expected to go to school, make good grades, and make my family proud. I was taught only education would help one escape from poverty.

My ancestors included Sir Truong-Nhu Cuong, who served several generations of Kings. Sir Truong-Nhu Cuong first served King Tu Duc in the nineteenth century and last served King Khai-Dinh in 1918, with his ranking as *Thuong Thu Bo Lai* or the equivalent of the Minister of Personnel Affairs in the modern system. King Khai Dinh was the father of Emperor Bao Dai, the last Vietnamese King whose regime ended in 1945.

My father, Sir Truong-Nhu Ngan, was two generations after Sir Truong-Nhu Cuong. He was born in 1900 and passed away in 1943, two years before the Royal regime was no longer active in Vietnam. My father used to work for the Nguyen Dynasty as *Tham Ta Toa Su*, the equivalent of Adviser Assistant for Ambassador in the modern system. I remember my father had his own escort whose job was to take him to work with a trishaw. My mother had two helpers to assist her. With my mother's supervision, the two helpers did most of the family's daily chores and cooked meals that catered to my father's tastes.

At only three years of age, I didn't understand enough to cry when my father passed away. On the day of his funeral, I innocently played in the yard and wondered why there were so many people in our house. I was too young to realize the loss and the sorrow my mother suffered.

Now I can't imagine how my mother managed to raise a family of six children without any help and without any career. I came to admire her even more when I saw how hard my wife Nga and I had to work to support our own family of six children. Generation after generation, Vietnamese women like my mother were taught to take care of the daily housewife duties, and many of them never had a chance for a formal education. The tradition of *Tai gia tong phu, xuat gia tong phu,* or "When you are at home, you serve your father; when you are married, you serve your husband" was the norm that many Vietnamese women inherited. When my father died, my mother was fairly young, but she never thought of herself — she always put our needs before her own. Starting at thirty-six years of age, my mother raised six of us; the oldest was ten, and the youngest was one. She managed to get all of us through school, at least high school.

In 1945, when the Japanese unconditionally surrendered to the Americans, starvation had killed over a million people in Northern Vietnam. For two long years, my mother had struggled to survive, to transform from a housewife to the head of the household — two long years of struggle and adaptation after my father passed away. At the time, I was five years old. I didn't understand the differences in economic status in Vietnamese society, but I knew my mother did the best she could to keep our family together. She ensured we received a decent education and had enough to eat and adequate clothes to wear.

During 1945, the British forces arrived in the southern city of Saigon to disarm the Japanese, and at the same time many poor Chinese nationalist peasants arrived in the northern city of Hanoi, also to disarm the Japanese. When Chinese troops agreed to withdraw from Vietnam and let the French return as a trade-off for French concessions in Chinese ports,

Ho Chi Minh welcomed the French in exchange for French recognition of his party, called the "Democratic Republic of Vietnam."

With the Japanese still in control of Indochina, King Bao Dai went along with a spontaneous non-communist meeting in Hanoi, which was against the French domination. Later I learned King Bao Dai had come to believe Ho Chi Minh and the Viet Minh were being helped by the Americans who could guarantee independence for Vietnam. When King Bao Dai was forced to abdicate by the Viet Minh in the North and thousands of Hue families adapted to the new social system, my family's status went through major changes.

Vietnam changed dramatically after the end of World War II. While South Vietnam was very uncertain due to the transformation of Royal society into a more Westernized society, the Northern part of Vietnam was mainly influenced by the Viet Minh. Living in Central Vietnam, in Hue City, my family was among thousands of civilians who witnessed the King's legacy and political changes. I didn't understand why we had such a huge difference in classification. While my siblings and I were fed very well by my mother with three meals a day, many children from North Vietnamese families starved to death. I didn't learn about the tragedies until my older brothers decided to become soldiers, and they taught me about the conflicts between communism and capitalism.

My parents had a large house, where the front living area was connected to the back by a walkway, with flowers in the double-side garden. The walkway and gardens were my favorite place because my mother and father had often relaxed there. Every month when the full moon appeared, my parents had sat in the garden to watch me play in the walkway. My mother said, "It was a peaceful and happy time."

When my father died, he had left my mother with no income to raise a family of six children. A housewife who did not know any form of business, my mother started selling everything she had accumulated over the years, including souvenir gold and family antique jewelry, to feed us. Without any further source of income, she couldn't afford to pay for the helpers anymore, so she took care of the chores herself. Several months after that, with little jewelry and gold left to sell, she had to put half of our house up for rent. We lived in the back of the house and rented out the front living area. My mother was very organized and had trained us to be neat. Although we did not have as much space as we were used to, she cleverly managed so all of us could fit in the back of the house comfortably.

The rental income enabled our family to survive for a couple more years. With time, more expenses were put on my mother's thin shoulders. The more the children grew, the more my mother struggled to feed and clothe us. Political chaos created more uncertainty for us and many others.

Where we lived in the Central area, most of the political events were mixed, half from Saigon and half from Hanoi. Hue people often had relatives who lived in each region; therefore, many were influenced by both Northern and Southern politics. Political propaganda from the North targeted peasants and less privileged classes of people, while in the South, Western influences became more popular.

When King Bao Dai resigned, the Viet Minh led by Ho Chi Minh, armed and supported by the French, systematically executed leaders and members of Vietnamese nationalist groups; their goal was to "wipe out the reactionaries." From the guise of nationalists, Viet Minh now officially indicated its agenda as communist. From 1946 to 1948, those considered dangerous to the Vietnamese Communist Party — including thousands of nationalists, Catholics, and others — were massacred by the Vietnamese communists, or Vietcong. It was very hard to distinguish who among the Viet Minh had become communists.

The threat by communism spread in Vietnam; King Bao Dai provoked war with the support of the French. After a series of violent clashes with the Vietcong, French forces bombarded Haiphong harbor and occupied Hanoi, forcing the Vietcong to retreat into the jungle. The political chaos became more dramatic when France took advantage of the uncertainty in Vietnam to establish its power in the Southeast region by supporting King Bao Dai with a series of conditions favorable for French colonialism. In 1948, France recognized an independent state of Vietnam and promoted King Bao Dai to be the Vietnamese leader. The new government with a new Vietnamese National Army was formed soon after.

Two years later, despite being defeated by the French and again by many Vietnamese nationalists including King Bao Dai, Ho Chi Minh was supported by China and the Soviet Union with his "Democratic Republic of Vietnam." I remember the talks between my brothers and my mother at the dining table. More than once, my mother stated it would break her heart if any of us participated in the political mess or joined the war. She didn't want to lose any of her children. My mother didn't like war; she wanted us to become ordinary citizens.

During these years, the lives of civilians in Hue were impacted deeply by the war. Utility costs rapidly increased. On top of daily expenses, the cost of education was unpredictable.

One day after dinner, my mother said, "I'm going to sell this house. I know it's hard, but I can't predict where the future will lead us."

"Mother," we all exclaimed. "What will we do?"

She answered, "We'll find another place to live. We need the money for you to continue with your educations."

We looked at each other in dismay.

"Anyway, once you have finished school, you should be

able to buy another property, perhaps even a better one."
We considered her words carefully. And then she said,
"The most important thing is for us to be together and support
each other. I would rather have less if all of you finish school."
As time passed, I realized my mother's hope was that when
we had finished school, Vietnam would be at peace, and we
would be able to build our own house.

We constantly moved from one place to another after
selling the house. First, my mother found a rental property in
Gia Hoi, separated from our old house by a river. This house
was convenient because it was close enough we could walk
to our school every day. However, we couldn't stay there very
long. At the time, there were no formal contracts for house
rental. The owners could ask for more money any time, and
if the renters could not afford the new payment, they had to
move.

A couple of months after we moved to Gia Hoi, the owner
began to increase the rental fees at almost every due date.
Unable to afford the increased cost, my mother searched for
a less expensive option, but most places were much further
from convenient school districts. We changed houses at least
four times during the next two years.

In Vietnam, people often joked that moving three times
would equal burning the house down one time. Worse than
having a burning house, my mother had no house to burn. I
don't know how she managed for six of us to continue our
education, while continuously on the move with such limited
resources. Perhaps people who lived during war time became
more determined and creative, like my mother, who passed
those traits on to me.

It was a difficult period for all of us. My mother made
every penny count for each of us. I learned to adapt to a new
school system almost every year, and I learned to make my
mother happy with my good academic records. My mother

did whatever was necessary to support us and keep the family going. Taking advantage of culture changes, where gold and jewelry values were more stable than currency, my mother became a businesswoman very quickly. She put her experience of saving and struggling as a housewife into business. With limited starting assets, she began buying gold at low cost and selling it when the price was higher.

My mother became very good at predicting gold values to maximize her profits. She established a small business at a local market, and our family's financial situation improved. My mother created a niche market for her local jewelry and gold exchange and developed a following of customers. With a much more stable income, my siblings and I were able to continue school and our lives became more comfortable. Almost ten years after my father died, my mother finally could pay the helpers again and support us with higher education. I admire my mother very much. She set an excellent example of hard work, determination, and creativity.

During the years when Vietnam was torn by so many conflicts, I was still very young and lucky to be the youngest. My two brothers were old enough to begin their college educations. From my brothers, I learned the Vietcong, which did not like the King's government, had been supported by Chinese and Russian communists. I was fourteen in 1954 when the French were defeated by the Vietcong.

My brother Tho told me about the Dien Bien Phu attack. He described a garrison organized by over 50,000 Vietcong who had dozens of battalions, groups of 75mm guns, and tanks — they outnumbered the French by nearly a five to one ratio. After the fall of Dien Bien Phu, more than 1,500 French had died along with over 8,000 Vietcong.

It was good to be independent, my brother Tho said, but it would be terrible if Vietnam followed communism. Tho was very patriotic, and he often told me how misleading the

Vietcong were. On the surface, the Vietcong used nationalism as their propaganda, but their final goal was to transform Vietnam into a communist country. My brothers did not like the communists, and they did not plan to become communists. My mother would always agree with my brothers Tho and Thung, but she did not want any of us to join the conflict.

After being defeated by the Vietcong, the French called on America and Britain for help in Southeast Asia. In 1954, the Geneva Conference was held, and the Geneva Accord, which divided Vietnam in half at the seventeenth parallel, was signed. The country was formally divided into the North, which belonged to the communists under Ho Chi Minh, and the South, under King Bao Dai, where freedom and independence were appreciated, but where a stable system of government had not yet been defined. 1954 was a sad year for Vietnam.

From August 1954 to May 1955, more than a million refugees fled south, while some 90,000 people from the south went north. At this same time, nearly 10,000 Vietcong were instructed by Hanoi to quietly remain behind in the South for a later propaganda agenda. Following the French departure from Hanoi, Ho Chi Minh returned to the North after eight years hiding in the jungle. In the South, King Bao Dai selected Mr. Ngo Dinh Diem as his prime minister. In October of 1954, President Eisenhower agreed to provide Mr. Ngo Dinh Diem with assistance directly, instead of channeling it through the French. Several months after this agreement, American aid was sent directly to South Vietnam. The U.S. government also offered to train the fledgling army. The South government started recruiting soldiers and officers to protect the South, and my brother Tho was among the first wave of South Vietnamese soldiers who volunteered.

Then, the first election in the South was held October 26, 1955, when the Republic of Vietnam (or South Vietnam) was declared with Mr. Ngo Dinh Diem as the President. This election was recognized by more than 100 countries.

That year, my mother's business slowed down because of the political events, and my oldest sister Tran decided to find administrative work to provide the family with supplemental income. My mother had a total of seven children. My oldest brother Cang died when he was only 4 years old, in 1931, before I was born. I have three sisters; my sister Tran, who is five years older than I, became the oldest when my brother died. With my father's death, Tran did not have the chance to go to college because she wanted to help my mother. I have always been close to Tran. Giao is 4 years younger than Tran and a year older than I, and my youngest sister Bich-Thuy, is 9 years younger than Tran.

I have two older brothers. After my brother Tho finished high school, he joined Da Lat Academy to become a South Vietnamese officer. When he left home for the academy, my mother cried so much. Tho assured my mother he would take good care of himself and make her proud. He added that when the country was at war, he could not stay home and watch. I always looked up to my brother Tho with admiration. He was a very good student, a great son, and a responsible citizen.

When he joined the South Vietnamese Army, Tho said, "I believe in human rights. Nationalism is very different from communism. The South Vietnamese have their rights to not follow communism."

Following Tho, my brother Thung and I also joined the South's military when we were called.

CHAPTER 4

# Mom: Childhood

My mother was born in a middle class family; both her parents were farmers. My grandparents' farming tradition influenced my mother's love of nature and living a simple life. My grandfather died at an early age, so my grandmother took charge and raised three children using her farming and small business skills around the village.

My mother grew up in My A, a small village far away from Hue and the Central Kingdom. She often went to the Tuy Van Pagoda when she was young. Tuy Van was a beautiful and historical pagoda, located on top of a hill in My A. My mother said she liked to climb up the hill as often as twice a month, just to enjoy the peaceful view of My A beneath the pagoda and to pray.

My parents married in 1920. My father was a clerk who worked at the Central Hospital, and my mother moved to Ben Ngu in Hue with him. On some special occasions, such as New Year or remembrance days of our ancestors, my parents took me and my other siblings to visit my grandma. From Ben Ngu where we lived, we had to travel almost half a day and pass a river called Pha Tam Giang to get to My A.

I remember the mysterious look of Pha Tam Giang and the legends the local people told us. One of these described a haunting from the depths of the dark, mysterious waters. People and boats disappeared from the banks and from the river, never to be seen again. Each time I sat in one of the small public boats that plied the river, I feared something bad would happen to us because my imagination reminded me of those tragic legends.

Perhaps I was born a worrier; I might have inherited this characteristic from my mother. She also used to worry a lot, maybe because she cared so much about everything she did.

I loved my mother very much. I remember the cozy feelings she created for our home. In 1930, my parents built their first and only house in Ben Ngu. It was a good-size house with many fruit trees in the back yard, but my favorite memories were the star fruit tree and a fish pond in the front yard.

I grew up in a beautiful time when my father worked at a local district agency and my mother was a stay-at-home housewife. She took care of us — from preparing the daily meals to washing our dirty clothes, from caring for the fruit trees to cleaning up the house. I remember many wonderful afternoon breaks with my mother, lying in the nest swing, looking up at the trees, having some star fruits, watching the fishes swimming in the pond, and falling into a short nap ... I loved seeing the fishes jumping above the water, and my mother often told me not to feed the fishes too much.

I was the youngest of five children, so I was also the most spoiled. My mother told us that school had been a luxury for her. My parents' wish was for us to have good educations and to have stable families of our own. I was sent to the Nam Giao Elementary School, adjacent to our house, when I was six.

Because I was a shy girl, I depended on my mother to walk me to school everyday. On rainy days, I found it hard to walk to class because I felt intimidated by the rain and the dark clouds. On those rainy days, Hue seemed pretty sad, partly because the winds and gray clouds made people feel depressed, and partly because the rain kept businesses from opening. On those dreary days, I felt safe holding my mother's hand, and the distance seemed much shorter when she was walking close to me.

In 1953, Hue suffered a heavy flood. Many houses in the area were destroyed by the storm and flood, and trees were heavily damaged. Many businesses were closed for more than a week. Fortunately, our house was on higher land, and the storm didn't destroy our neighborhood.

In Ben Ngu, there was no electricity and transportation was disrupted, so there was no school. I was still a silly kid who liked to join others to play in the flood water, too young to realize how much trouble I caused my mother. After several hours playing in dirty water, I went home, changed clothes, and went to sleep.

The next morning, I couldn't get up because of severe flu and fever. My head was so hot it felt like it was on fire! I remember my mother touching my forehead. She diagnosed that I had a fever and wondered if I stayed outdoors while she was working in the garden. My mother didn't raise her voice or complain. She just quietly cooked me some chicken soup and dosed me with medicine three times a day. A couple of days later, I could join the other kids on the first day school reopened after the flood.

Seeing the sadness in my mother's face, I felt guilty because I'd disappointed her. I told her I was so sorry and I would listen to her when she said not to play with dirty water anymore. I promised to make it up to her by being a good daughter.

This incident reminded me of how patient my mother was, and I learned not to upset nor disappoint her. I vowed that I would focus my energy on studying so she would be very proud of me. From an early age, I learned my mother had given herself to raise our family. She was a strong woman who I admired very much.

Although I didn't finish college as my mother wished, I've tried my best not to disappoint her. Naturally, when I was first pregnant, my wishes were for all my children to graduate from college, to marry good citizens, and to find good jobs to support their own families.

In 1954, when I was eight years old, I saw my mother crying. I didn't understand what made her so sad. She stayed sad for months. Later, she told me that she didn't believe in the zodiac, but she had to believe people had their own fortune, especially after what happened to my two oldest brothers. I had three brothers and a sister at the time. My mother told me that my two oldest brothers, Anh Hai and Anh Ba, ran away from home, and that I might not see them again.

Anh Hai and Anh Ba broke my mother's heart. It wasn't until we left Vietnam more than twenty years later that I learned why my brothers had run away. Although we had the same roots, my brothers burned the connection to our family by joining the Vietcong. My mother chose to stay in Vietnam to have a chance to see them again.

At the time, I didn't know how to react to my mother's decision. I was naive, too naive to understand how communist propaganda could affect my family. I was naive, too naive to pay attention to politics, too naive to make a difference in my mother's life. I was a housewife who didn't have much interest in politics. I didn't know how to persuade my mother to leave Vietnam with us.

I had to leave my mother to start a new life for my family; there was no better way once Vietnam fell into communism. Ironically, my husband was a South Vietnamese officer whose stand was in direct opposition to my brothers and the communists. My heart was broken when I left Vietnam; however, I believe I made the right decision to leave.

I learned another reason for my mother to stay in Vietnam was to be with my older sister Le and her family. Six years older than me, like my mother, my sister Le did not have the luxury of finishing school. In 1954, when Anh Hai and Anh Ba left our family, my parents depended on my sister Le for many daily chores. I was the most spoiled kid in my family, partly because I was the youngest, but mostly because of my sister Le.

When Le was young, she refused many opportunities to date because she wanted to stay with my parents to help them raise the family. Sister Le helped my parents without questioning what her privileges were. She was a loving sister who was very handy and worked extremely hard. Le finally dated when she was twenty-four and got married two years later to her only love.

When Le started dating, I was afraid to lose her to my brother-in-law, and I often showed my jealousy when my future brother-in-law came to visit us. Later when they got married, they stayed with my parents and continued to help support me and my brother for a while. I was wrong for being jealous because Le always showed me how much she loved me. In addition, my brother-in-law was a very down-to-earth and supportive person, and I came to consider him my actual brother.

In Vietnam, the family grew in size when the children got married. In many cases, one big family could consist of three to five sub-families, and everyone stayed in the same house with different rooms. We had a big family, and having my sister Le and her husband staying in my mother's house helped my mother. They took good care of her when my father died.

Sister Le was truly a Vietnamese housewife. Every day she cleaned, cooked, and helped my mother with many daily chores without complaining. The older I get, the more I appreciate what she did for me. I could go to the Ham Long High School, which was located in Bao Quoc Pagoda's land, because my sister Le had left her school to help my parents to support us. While I was enjoying my favorite history and geography lessons at Ham Long, my sister worked hard to earn supplemental income for our family. She convinced my father to retire. She told my parents it was time for them to rest, and because she would be able to help, they wouldn't be so worried about the future.

Sister Le was two years older than my third brother Thao, who was a handsome man and very athletic. I was very proud to walk with him to school because he was not only an excellent student but also a great volleyball player.

My brother Thao died when he was twenty years old from heartache. Local people gossiped that Thao died because of being "love-sick," a common "syndrome" that many Westernized Vietnamese students often claimed, like the "hippie" time in America during the 60s. Thao passed away without fulfilling the hopes of my parents. It took my parents a long time to overcome this sad news.

After I was married, my husband disclosed to me that he was Thao's classmate, and when Thao died, he had been one of the guests at the funeral. We did not know about each other at the time. It was a surprising coincidence for me!

Our sorrows were then lessening after so much dramatic chaos had happened to Vietnam. My family, like many others, was scattered by the winds of communism.

CHAPTER 5

# Dad: The Happiness and the Loss of a Young Vietnamese Academic

I was very lucky to be the youngest son of my mother. When all of my elder siblings married and started families of their own, I stayed with my mother and my little sister Bich-Thuy. My mother and I went through a lot together, especially when Bich-Thuy passed away.

Bich-Thuy died when she was eighteen years old — possibly from chickenpox, but we don't know for sure. The medical treatment in Vietnam was not sophisticated at the time. Within five days of being admitted to the hospital, she passed away without a definitive diagnosis. My mother broke down for months after that. I loved my sister Bich-Thuy very much; she was sweet and caring, and I grieved at the shortness of her life.

It hurt to see my mother's pain, while she constantly worried about my brothers — and later me — who had joined the South Vietnamese military forces. My mother told us if we continued in the military, she would lose us one by one to the Vietcong. My mother had no choices. Even though she expressed her unwillingness for us to join the military, she understood what life would be like if the South was ruled by communists. Her mother's instinct told her as long as one of us was in the front line, she faced the possibility of losing a son. Many days while my brothers Thung and Tho were in training or camping, she stayed home and prayed to Buddha to save them.

In contrast to my older brothers, I wasn't actively involved in politics. Not until my brothers were killed and I witnessed many family tragedies did I voluntarily begin to support the war.

After passing the *Tu Tai 2* or "high school-second part" national exam, I was accepted to college and earned my bachelor's degree in science, majoring in *Toan-Ly-Hoa*, or Mathematics-Physics-Chemistry concentration. With a certification equivalent to a bachelor's degree, I started my teaching career in Ham Long and semi-private high schools in Hue.

I had a simple life. As a teacher, I started my day at seven in the morning and went home around four in the afternoon. From the day my youngest sister died, my mother and I were very close. I became the youngest child, and my mother was unwilling to let me go. She counted on me to deal with her emotional stress, and in return, she showered me with attention and care. To help my mother's stress, I learned to remain calm and be a good listener.

I called my mother Mo, and Mo took great care of me until I graduated from college. When I got my first job as a teacher, it was time for Mo to relax and retire at home. She was very traditional and kept asking me to get married and have children so she could spoil her *chau noi* or "grandchildren from the son." My mother wished to live long enough to see my children grow up. She wanted us to keep the Truong-Nhu tradition. When my brothers Tho and Thung died, their families stayed with us. I had a big extended family. After all of my siblings had families of their own, my mother often questioned if I had any dates yet. I believe in the zodiac of life. I believe Buddha blessed me to find Nga among many ladies from Hue. From the first time I met her, I knew Nga was the one for me and it was time for me to start a family. After two years of following Vietnamese tradition and custom, I officially asked Nga to be my wife, and I believe that was the happiest day of my life. During the most difficult years in Vietnam, I had my most two important women by my side: my mother and my loving wife Nga. I am glad Nga learned to love my mother as her own and both Nga and I were there to support my mother, as my mother had been there for me since the day my father died.

I told Nga that perhaps my mother was so strict because she had been through many difficult times in her life, and she was very persistent and disciplined. She was quite protective, and at first Nga found it challenging to adapt to my mother's traditions. Nga was always very supportive and respected my mother and understood her protectiveness. With Cang's death, followed by my father's death in 1943 due to stomach cancer, then my sister Bich-Thuy's death in 1961, my mother was very conscious of the transience of life and the ever-present possibility of death.

## CHAPTER 6

# Mom: Growing Up, Falling in Love, and Becoming a Housewife

In high school, I liked history and geography though I felt intimidated by science. But my physics and math instructor in my last year of high school, 1963-1964, changed that. He set my heart beating faster and made me feel like I was having trouble breathing ... and not because I was intimidated by the math and physics!

Like many other instructors in Vietnam, Dinh was a strict and serious teacher, respected by his students. I admired and adored him at the same time.

There were three outgoing girls in Dinh's class: my two best friends, Hanh and Chieu, and I. We often told funny jokes, and Dinh liked our senses of humor. One day, because we had done very well in responding to questions in class, teacher Dinh rewarded us by inviting us for some luncheon snacks after school. We accepted the invitation, and I was thrilled that with three girls to choose among, he sat next to me when we went out to Banh Beo Vy Da, a famous place in Hue that served a special Banh Beo dish!

After the luncheon, I could feel something special between us — the way we looked at each other could not be a simple teacher-student relationship! Like a typical daydreaming high school girl, I thought of Dinh constantly. Distracted by his image, I couldn't concentrate on my school work.

He was very special to me, and I could tell he liked me very much, too. His manners showed it all. He paid more attention to the way he talked and directed questions to me. I was so happy just to chat randomly with him at school, but I trembled inside each time he offered me a drink or lent me a book. One day, Dinh finally asked if he could visit me at home.

According to Vietnamese tradition, if a gentleman wanted to date a girl, he often showed his interest by paying a formal visit to the house to ask her parents for approval. When Dinh asked me for a proper time to visit my home, I wanted to jump up and down for joy, but making the arrangement proved very difficult. I had to use all my powers of persuasion to convince my father to allow me to develop a relationship while I was in high school. After several cancellations, my father finally agreed to meet Dinh.

Dinh came to our home for the first time, neatly dressed in a white shirt and dress pants. His appearance and manners won my parents' hearts, and we started to date officially, requiring that I transfer to different school.

We have many great memories about our dating time: walks along the river, special food in special places, and visits to many historical places in Hue. The best of all was the first time I met Dinh's family. I was as nervous at this first time visit as if I were taking a physics exam. I said very little, watched my manners, and spoke only when asked a question.

At that time, if you didn't win the hearts of your future in-laws, it was hard to talk about marriage! Thank goodness both Dinh and I had our parents' approval. We were lucky because both families were pretty much open to Western influence. We had the chance to meet and learn about each other before the marriage instead of entering into an arranged marriage like many others who lived in the countryside.

At the time, the typical age of marriage for Vietnamese girls was about eighteen to twenty. A woman over thirty could be considered too old for marriage.

Dinh and I married on June 20, 1965, after a memorable year of preparation and growing love. We were blessed to have our marriage witnessed by many family members, friends, and close relatives.

I respected my husband for being such a gentleman and such a kind person. During the time we dated, Dinh proved that he was a very noble and educated person. He protected me and respected me very much. He saved our magical moment for the wedding day, and this made us very special.

I like the Vietnamese proverb that says, *Tuong Kinh Nhu Tan*, or "We always respect each other, as the first time we met." This proverb has been with us for many years, whether we are in our up or down times of life. I hope my children will learn this proverb and keep the tradition.

When I first joined Dinh's family, I was too nervous to be myself because I didn't have any experience at being a house-wife. Traditionally, newlyweds stayed with the husband's family, and the wife had to follow his family's traditions. If the husband's family turned out to be very difficult, it would be hard for the bride to adapt. I was fortunate Dinh's family was such a loving family, and everyone welcomed me with open arms.

My mother-in-law, my husband's brother Anh Tho, Anh Tho's wife, and his four children all lived with us. We had a big family! I'll never forget how nervous I was when I sat at the family dining table for the first time! I couldn't start a conversation because I was so shy.

For weeks, my husband had to find snacks for me at night, because I couldn't eat much at the table, partly because I was shy and partly because I missed my mother's food so much! Some days at dinner time, I was so emotional I couldn't even taste the food. Starting my own life apart from my mother proved to be a challenging task for me. I'm so glad my husband was patient and helped me to be independent.

Luckily, I had a good mother-in-law; she was pretty easygoing, and she took care of most of the family's business. Although her mind set was traditional, she treated me politely and fairly. Unlike the way many Vietnamese brides were treated in other families, my mother-in-law did not give me a hard time.

Ten months after Dinh and I married, our first daughter Ngoc was born. My mother-in-law loved Ngoc very much and was pleased with how much she looked like Dinh. I felt more comfortable with my new life, but I still visited my mother when I could.

I learned to cook; cared for my child; and did the typical housework duties, such as cleaning and washing clothes. I strived to set a good example of being polite, and I came to love my husband's mother as I loved my own.

Then, I started running Dinh's family business: selling rice as the war had made commodities more valuable than luxuries. When the business went well, my mother-in-law hired a couple of workers to help us expand the business and to handle daily chores for me. I had a comfortable life, and we had a big and happy family.

CHAPTER 7

# Dad: "Xep But Nghieng Theo Viec Dao Binh," or "Put the Book Aside, Follow the Call of Your Country at War"

My youth was immersed in news and tragedies from the war.

I got married in 1965, when the US helped the South Army and pressured the North into a negotiation for peace. During 1965 and 1966, I delayed my reporting to Thu Duc Academy to stay home to take care of my mother and Nga. I was in the reserve unit and was called to be in the army in November 1966, several months before my brother Tho died. I personally didn't want to be at the front line like my brothers, not because I was weak or afraid of death, but because I realized how much my mother and my family needed me since we had lost my two older brothers.

By the end of 1965, an estimated 90,000 South Vietnamese soldiers had deserted, with the US troop levels in Vietnam reaching over 180,000. Like most of my Vietnamese colleagues,

I didn't know that more than 35,000 Vietcong had infiltrated the South via the Ho Chi Minh Trail. Like most of my South Vietnamese colleagues, I didn't know that almost fifty percent of the countryside in the South was then under some degree of Vietcong control.

From 1964 to 1966, many South Vietnamese families suffered the same losses we did. The Vietcong were very unpredictable, and we could see bad news happening everywhere. A couple of months after my brother Tho died, the fighting between the North and the South worsened. The South was supported by the Americans, and bombing in Hanoi started in April 1966. The North attacked many areas in Saigon and its suburbs, causing hundreds of casualties and destroying many American helicopters and aircraft.

1966 was a remarkable year for me, a turning point. It was the year I started my own family with Nga, the year we had our first daughter — and it was the year my loving brother Thung was shot down by the communists. The reality hit me so powerfully and, for the first time, as a high school teacher, I felt the impact of the war on my own family. When my nation was invaded, it was almost impossible to protect my family and my personal treasures. Despite my mother's unwillingness for me to join the war, I registered to be in the national reserve forces.

As a young recruit, I listened to the news and wondered what the future held for the South. At the end of 1966, President Johnson conducted a conference in Manila with his allies, including Australia, Philippines, Thailand, New Zealand, South Korea, and South Vietnam. The allies pledged to withdraw from Vietnam within six months if North Vietnam would withdraw completely from the South. America was under pressure to withdraw from Vietnam, while South Vietnamese officers were caught between fighting for their country and Vietcong propaganda.

I had learned from my brothers that the Vietcong were very tricky in their tactics. Because there were so many under-cover Vietcong within the South, especially in the country-side, it was hard for us to identify our enemies. It wasn't a fair fight —America publicized its aid for the South, while the North quietly searched for its support from China and Russia.

My brother Tho had told me that there were cases when the Vietcong avoided the fight and retreated into the jungle, leaving the South troops to uncover and destroy an extensive network of their tunnels. After the American and South Vietnamese troops left the area, the Vietcong would return and rebuild their sanctuary. This pattern was repeated throughout the war, and the Americans advised soldiers like my brothers Thung and Tho to utilize in-and-out tactics, in which the troops arrived in the suspect area by helicopters, secured the area, then departed by helicopters.

Throughout the years, I learned of so many tragedies of Vietnam. I learned that French Indochina's rules were replaced by the fascism of Japan. I learned about the starvation of millions of Vietnamese in the North under Japanese exploita-tion during World War II and realized how effective the Vietcong propaganda was. It was very sad, after a thousand years, that Vietnam was still divided by different opinions; after so many diversified influences from the world, the Vietcong still believed that communism was the best for the Vietnamese. I disagreed with this.

I learned that after 1954, many innocent Vietnamese were executed in the North. The Vietcong had brainwashed followers to testify against family members and others who had more education and wealth than the rest. I learned about the *Cai Cach Ruong Dat* or the Land Reform Act in the North, when thousands of educators, teachers, engineers, and land-lords were executed. I learned there was no such thing as indi-vidualism in the North, where socialism was the norm —

where they believed there was no better idealism than communism.

Throughout the years of witnessing Vietnamese history, I discovered many things for which I was willing to fight. I learned my two brothers, Tho and Thung, had died for a good cause. I had their honorable examples, and my family's safety to protect. I was no longer a young Vietnamese academic.

### 

It was 1965. Many Vietnamese academics like me had quit our civilian jobs to join the South Army. I can still remember the words in President Johnson's speech broadcast on the daily news:

*"For centuries, nations have struggled among each other. But we dream of a world where disputes are settled by law and reason. And we will try to make it so.*

*"For most of history men have hated and killed one another in battle. But we dream of an end to war. And we will try to make it so.*

*"For all existence most men have lived in poverty, threatened by hunger. But we dream of a world where all are fed and charged with hope. And we will help to make it so."*

Yes, my brothers Tho and Thung dreamed of a world where all were fed and charged with hope. All of us dreamed of an end to war, but before we could fulfill our dream, we had to deal with the reality — a reality where reasoning wasn't enough to convince our enemies and where enemies' propaganda was too effective to stop. After a couple years' delay due to my marriage and helping my mother, I finally made up my mind. I found a perfect balance of supporting the war and taking care of my family by joining the Thu Duc Academy, the national reserve army school, in November of 1966.

November was the cold season in Hue, and the weather

made me even sadder when I left home for the academy. I was transferred to a DaNang camp after initial registration, along with many other new cadets. I missed Hue, my elderly mother, and my loving wife, who was a couple of months pregnant. Each time I saw a little baby who lived near the camp, I thought of my own baby Ngoc, who was less than a year old, and wished for the nine months of my training to speed by. I couldn't eat much during the days or sleep well at nights from worry about the safety of my family. My first week in DaNang was extremely hard because I had little to do and lots of time to think of my family.

After the first week, I was transported by air to Saigon; Thu Duc Academy was located about twenty kilometers away from Saigon. The schools, the Thu Duc Infantry Reserve Officers School and its sister school in Nam Dinh in North Vietnam, were established in October 1951. Both schools were originally administered by the French Army, and most students were sent to France to complete the training. When the Nam Dinh School was closed in 1952, the Thu Duc Academy became the only school that produced reserve officers.

After the Geneva Accord was signed in 1954, the school changed its management from French to South Vietnamese Armed Forces. After 1955, the Thu Duc Academy trained cadres and specialists of other branches for the South Army in addition to the infantry. In July 1964, Thu Duc Academy was officially named the Infantry School, and the cadet population had grown to almost four thousand. Thu Duc Academy was considered one of the most important military installations in South Vietnam during the war. By 1966, the school maintained one class per year, and the training lasted from nine months to two years, depending upon the corps' specifications.

I was a little nervous traveling by bus from the airport to the Academy. Looking out the windows, I could see many greeters standing along the campus — ladies in *ao dai* reminded me of home in Hue, and I felt Nga's absence as if a part of me was missing. The cheerful attitude of the Saigon people and the upbeat scenarios reminded me of how quiet Hue was.

The bus stopped at the gate, where a large logo reflected the bright sunlight, *Truong Si Quan Thu Duc*, or Thu Duc Reserve Infantry School. The Academy's logo, big and bold in front of the new cadets on buses, marked the time to start a new life — less personal, more disciplined, and very realistic.

The first week at Thu Duc Academy was an interesting one. Trainee-cadets like me stood in line for uniforms and army personal supplies. I had my hair done by the military barber. Everyone had the same haircut, about a quarter-inch long. Everyone was grouped by individual squad and platoon. Luckily, I was grouped with several trainee-cadets from Hue; and within a couple of days, we were very open with each other; and I could start many good conversations.

I was admitted to the Academy when the school had initiated a change in the training curriculum. To meet the increased demand for general mobilization and military officers, the length of the officer candidate program was shortened from almost two years to about thirty-seven weeks. The first eight weeks consisted of basic and advanced individual training at the Quang Trung Training Center. The rest of the training was often conducted at the school, where each cadet could select his own area of concentration.

Basic and advanced individual training were very strict. All trainee cadets had to follow a fixed agenda, including exercise and body training each day. For most of the time, cadets like me were taught to follow directions without questioning. During the days, I was too busy to feel the depth of my sadness or to worry about my family. At night, everyone was exhausted and didn't have time to think of his civilian life. But when I looked at Ngoc's and Nga's pictures in my wallet, I wished I could see them.

Eight weeks flashed by like a hurricane passing through a tropical area — faster than I could imagine. Through military training, I gained more confidence and surprised myself at how tough I could be. All the trainee cadets who passed the initial training were officially accepted as officer cadets and received two days of vacation. I participated in the "Alpha pin ceremony" held at the school for new officer cadets, and I felt so much pride to wear the Academy uniform. Eight weeks of very hard work and learning actually paid off.

I was so proud to graduate from Thu Duc Academy — proud of the opportunity to give back to my country, proud of the fact I understood, for the first time, the value of being proactive. I had learned more about world history and more about Vietnam's position in the world.

I understood the objectives of the academy, illustrated by its logo: The blue background represented the pure form of mind and actions and reminded gentlemen about their responsibilities to their country; the red flame represented consistency, giving, and bravery; and the sword represented leadership and honor. There were four words on the logo, *Cu An Tu Nguy*, or "Live with peace, but do not underestimate the threat." These words came from Lam Son, a senior grade officer who had made significant contributions to the South Army with his philosophy and wisdom.

Once I passed the initial training, the following months were much easier. I was transferred to Saigon to finish my specialized concentration, which was Military Supplies, or Quartermaster.

My mother's instinct that she would lose more of her children was accurate. Five years after my sister Bich-Thuy died, my mother received the sad news about my brother Thung. Thung was very studious and the pride of my mother. He graduated from college and became an instructor at the Quoc Hoc Institute in Hue, where he taught math and science. Thung was called to be in a reserve unit for military training. He joined Thu Duc Academy for one year and graduated from the academy as an Artillery Observer Officer for the South Vietnamese Air Force. Thung was a true gentleman who mastered the cultures of both West and East. He was very responsible and had a strong work ethic.

Thung was an experienced artillery observer officer who volunteered to substitute for a sick teammate, not for the first time. He had told my mother just a day earlier he would soon be on vacation and would take her out for dinner when he saw her. Even though prepared for possible loss during war, Thung's death on February 20th, 1966, shocked my mother because she expected him to be coming home for vacation, not flying on Observation Flight L19. But due to a shortage on the observation team, he volunteered to help out, and Thung and other officers on the flight were shot down by the Vietcong. He never made it home to see our mother, his beautiful wife, or his two precious daughters, much to the sorrow of all of us.

We had a big extended and very close family. My mother was strong as she always expressed her determination to be the adviser for everyone at home. After Thung died, my mother became stricter. She often reminded us, "Always be close to each other and help out when needed."

Almost a year went by. My brother Tho was promoted to Head of the Third Regiment, under the First Infantry Division. He was the subordinate of the Division's Lieutenant General, who was among top ranking officers primarily responsible for the security of the South forces.

My mother was still very cautious. It took a while to convince her to let Nga go to Saigon the first time to see me. My mother told us, "It's dangerous, and if something bad happened, I'd rather have the family together."

Finally, she agreed Nga could go to Saigon to see me, but my mother's instinct was correct. Even before we had a chance to begin seeing the sights of Saigon, we received word of Tho's death and were called home for the funeral.

On June 4, 1967, as Tho slept within his military camp near Hue's suburbs, he was attacked by a group of Vietcong. These Vietcong, according to the local investigators, had broken through a barbed wire fence along the camp and used guns with silencers to execute him during his sleep. No trace of the executioners was ever found, but at the same time Tho died, his private driver disappeared.

Later, after I emigrated to the United States, I realized what happened to my brother Tho was not unusual during the Vietnam War. Like many other Vietnamese communists who stayed in the South after the Geneva Accord, Tho's private driver was an undercover Vietcong. When he disappeared after my brother's execution, he probably went back into the jungle to join his troops.

My brother Tho was honored with a national military ceremony at his funeral. In addition to his beloved family, friends, and neighbors, mourners included the Division's Lieutenant General and military personnel from other high ranking officers to cadets. I can still remember the ceremony day when his closed coffin was covered with the South Vietnam national flag. The yellow base and three red stripes of the flag provided a vivid reminder of blood shed in the sunlight of the fallen warrior's life. Tho's uniformed subordinates displayed respect and admiration from the first notes of the national anthem to the conclusion of the national funeral procession for the South Vietnamese Army hero. His coffin, escorted by young soldiers and honor cadets, was placed in the Combat Vehicle M113 for its final journey.

Tho's death pushed my mother's suffering to the highest

state of sorrow. She looked at my brothers' pictures and cried. She had lost two of her sons to the communists in only sixteen months. Tho and Thung left my mother with their legacies, Tho had four children and Thung had two — a total of six innocent kids left fatherless by the Vietcong.

There was a huge hole in our family. I can still remember my mother's stricken face. Her walk was weak, unbalanced, and depressed. Everything about her spoke of desolation. Pain stabbed my chest when I saw Tho's proper wife and his four little children in the traditional white funeral uniform. My beloved Nga's face was filled with sadness also. For the whole week, I suffered, not only from the loss of my heroic older brother but also from my powerlessness to comfort any of my family. A huge hole had been ripped in the fabric of our lives — an immense loss for all of us.

My mother developed insecure feelings after losing her sons. She was terrified and clung to me, afraid to let me go each time I was called for military duties. Every day, she reminded me in a tiny voice, "Be extremely careful. You are the only son I have left. I just won't be able to make it if something bad happens to you."

Then while the pain was still a fresh and throbbing ache in our hearts, it was time for me to go back to training in Saigon. I said goodbye to my mother, Nga and my baby Ngoc, and other members in the family and returned to duty. I supported the war, not only because of the loss of my brothers, but also because I knew we had to fight for freedom. Without freedom, we could not have a peaceful life.

Yes, there is a price for everything. I never took life for granted after my brothers' deaths. I believed we needed to fight for life. I needed to go back to military training in Thu Duc Academy, and I needed to fulfill my duties as a soldier.

My two brothers' deaths gave me the privilege of serving as a Quartermaster, which meant I didn't have to be at the front line. If I had to choose a military pathway again, I would make the same decision to become a Quartermaster. It was good for my family and suitable for my academic record, and it also honored my brothers and supported my country.

I graduated from Thu Duc Academy with Aspirant, or Third Lieutenant, ranking in late November 1967. 1966 and 1967 were emotional years for me. At twenty-six years old, I was mature enough to realize how complicated Vietnamese history was. I learned to accept the brutal fact of history — that conflicts constantly occur, not only between enemies but also within parties and people who have the same goals. It was sad.

One could easily see how hard it would be for a soldier to fight when he did not have his country's support. Even though I wished the Americans had remained to help the South Vietnamese like me fight the war, I understood how problematic it could have been for them to stay longer. I recognized people must take care of themselves first before they can help others, but it was difficult to see them go. I also realized the immense importance of my family. Without their support, it would have been impossible for me to fight this war — or any war.

After graduation, I was anxious to see my family. Rather than waiting for a military truck to Hue, I purchased an airline ticket to get home as soon as I could. Nine months was far too long to be away. Although I had gone back to attend my brother Tho's funeral, that occasion had been deeply sorrowful, and I didn't have time to socialize with my local friends or to visit my relatives. The training had been so hectic I didn't have any time to spend with Nga, who had given birth to our second child Phuc in August of 1967.

When I arrived home after my training was complete, Nga and Ngoc greeted me at the airport. We stayed in my mother's new house, which had been provided by the South government after my brother Tho died. When I had been away, my mother had insisted Nga stay with her. I was glad Nga and I were very close to my mother, so they could take care of each other while I was away for camps or military duties.

However, Nga found it difficult to be dependent on my mother. Naturally, my wife liked to have her independent space, but she understood how protective my mother was, considering how conscious she was about the transience of life. I convinced Nga it was necessary for us to be there for our mothers, especially while Vietnam suffered so many conflicts.

Over time, Nga became comfortable with the family traditions and helped my mother with the rice business. Even better, my mother-in-law lived fairly close by, and Nga and she visited frequently. At least several times a week, we had dinners and lunches with my mother-in-law. Sometimes, we were able to invite both our mothers for extended family dinners. Both grandmothers played important roles in the lives of Ngoc and Phuc. Life was not bad at this time.

For my first duty station, I reported to the First Company in Mang Ca, Hue as a Quartermaster. My responsibilities included the distribution of gas and military supplies for the First Infantry Division. I managed about ten financial officers and accountants. Though my job duties were not as challenging as being at the front line, they involved much planning and communications. I finally could put my years of academic math and science skills to practical use managing the facility and gas supply in Mang Ca.

## CHAPTER 8

# Mom: Dinh Is Called Up

When Ngoc was ten months old, my husband, who was in the national reserve unit, was called to serve in the South Vietnam military service. Dinh hadn't been on active duty lists for a couple of years because of the death of his older brother, Anh Thung; he had to go this time.

Anh Thung had been a pilot in the South Vietnamese Air Force. He died in combat with the Vietcong in 1966, several months after we got married. Anh Thung left behind his wife and two daughters.

My husband had to close his science books and learn more about military terminologies and techniques. When the nation was at risk, he had to serve. Dinh was sent to Saigon, to the Thu Duc Academy for training. Without my husband, I felt as if the best part of Hue had disappeared. Although I had my in-laws with me, I missed my husband and felt alone without him. I tried to focus on the family business to fill the long and lonely days.

Saigon, the capital of South Vietnam, was a large, growing city, more diverse with a higher standard of living than other cities in Vietnam. In contrast to the people of Hue, people in

Saigon were generally more friendly and outgoing. Dinh told me Saigon was called "the Pearl of Southeast Asia" because of its rich cultural environment. Saigon had been westernized from French Colonial influences, and then more rapidly changed by the United States' military bases.

I'd always wanted to see the modern developments of Saigon, so the chance to visit my husband while he was attending the military training thrilled me.

Taxis and cars sped down the streets; people drove cars to work; whereas, in Hue, we rode bicycles and used cars only on special occasions. I saw young girls with short hair wearing shirts and pants, while girls in Hue typically wore their hair long and straight and dressed in traditional *ao dai* (a long Vietnamese dress). Saigon's fast pace and multiple colors excited me.

On the second day I was in Saigon, we received a telegram from my mother-in-law telling us Anh Tho died during combat with the Vietcong. Anh Tho, Dinh's second older brother, was a lieutenant-colonel in the South Vietnamese Army. Another family member killed by the Vietcong!

We returned to Hue without visiting the modern places I'd looked forward to seeing in Saigon. After the national ceremony and family funeral for Anh Tho, I once again told Dinh goodbye. He returned to training in Saigon, and his mother and I returned to sadness and loneliness.

My mother-in-law had seven children, and she had lost two in tragedies before adulthood. Now, two of her sons had been killed by the communists. After Anh Tho died, my husband was the only son she had left. I can't begin to describe how sad she was — the loss of a child creates a deep, painful wound that never heals, and my mother-in-law felt this pain for the fourth time. I wanted so much to ease her pain, but nothing can heal the wound of a mother's loss. And I was feeling so lonely with Dinh in Saigon — it seemed like he was in another world because he wasn't with me.

In Saigon, Dinh went through basic military training for four months, and then he was transferred to the specialized Military Supply Division, where he wouldn't have to go into combat or be at the frontline.

Dinh told me, "There is a price for everything. According to South Vietnamese Government law, I have the privilege to stay with the family, to take care of you and our children, and to care for my mother. But I can do this only because my two brave brothers are no longer alive."

After nine months' training Dinh came back to Hue as a South Vietnamese officer, stationed at the camp in Mang Ca, Hue.

While my husband fulfilled his assignment in Hue in Su Doan I Bo Binh, the first Infantry Division, my son Phuc was born in 1967. He was six months old when the Vietnamese Lunar New Year, the Year of the Monkey, 1968, arrived.

CHAPTER 9

# Dad: The Personal Story of a South Vietnamese Military Officer

I managed several gas warehouses in Mang Ca in addition to several stockrooms in Quang Tri and Dong Ha provinces near the seventeenth parallel. I had to send guards and observe the operations of all these gas supply facilities. One time, on a routine trip to Quang Tri and Dong Ha, my subordinate Chien and I had a car accident on the slippery road. The Jeep turned upside down in a tropical storm, but thanks to Buddha's blessing, we both avoided calamity and returned home safely to our families.

As the war became more active, my work started getting harder. I often went to work early and came home late. Some days, if the distribution schedule was slowed as a result of traffic regulations or war demands, I stayed at the camp where the gas supplies were. To catch up with dynamic movements and changes the war imposed on an immature government, the

South Vietnamese military underwent major re-organization. Within two years, my unit experienced many changes.

Besides managing gas supplies, I was assigned the responsibility for other military supplies such as uniforms and telecommunication equipment. My unit also had more headcounts and received help directly from the American advisors. During this time, I often interacted with an American soldier whose last name was Woods. I don't remember his first name since I always called him Mr. Woods. He was a sergeant major at the time he worked with me.

Mr. Woods was really kind and funny. Any time I needed help to move supplies to mountain areas where cargo couldn't be shipped directly, he was always available to help. He often coordinated helicopters to move supplies and food to military units in the jungle. As I remember, Mr. Woods was married and had a son about two or three years old. He showed me his family pictures during breaks and often asked me how my family was.

Mr. Woods frequently brought candies and American magazines to our families. Occasionally, he took me and two other officers to watch the shows that entertained American soldiers. I've never forgotten him with his sense of humor and the caring things he did for our family. When my wife Nga had our third baby Thuy, Mr. Woods paid us a formal visit at our home, bringing a lot of American gifts — baby clothes and toys. Nga has often asked me to search for him because she always remembers his generosity and kindness.

For several years after I came to America in 1975, I searched for him with no success. Mr. Woods, if you read these lines, I hope you remember the friendship you brought to my family and to Vietnam. I cherish your kindness and will never forget the short time I interacted with you. Your camp was located on the opposite side of my unit, across the *Song Huong* River or Perfume River, next to the Vietnamese

General's house at the time. Please, contact me if you read this book and see your image in these lines!

And while Mr. Woods is the individual who meant so much to me and my family, he is a symbol of many American soldiers who extended friendship and kindness to many South Vietnamese officers and their families during those war years. I thank them all.

Our unit moved to Gia Le in 1972, when the rumor spread that it was time for Americans to withdraw from Vietnam. It was a very challenging time for all of us, and my duties increased without much outside support. Our offices moved into a temporary space away from the warehouse, and I had to drive much further to work.

Because of the longer distance from home, it was hard for me to commute every day. So I stayed at the unit and had just one day a week to visit my family. I left Nga at home to take care of the children since I didn't have any other choice.

About a year after I moved my office to Gia Le, I was promoted to auditor, and the work became busier. As my life became more involved with daily military duties, I cherished every moment I had with my family. When I was sent to Saigon for twelve weeks for training, saying goodbye to Nga, my children, and my mother was very painful. Leaving them in Hue during my training ripped another hole in my bruised heart because we had experienced firsthand the brutal uncertainty of life during the war and because we didn't know what awaited us in the future.

But the time eventually passed, and I assumed another position in DaNang. Once again, I experienced a life full of conflict and contradiction. As before, I lived at work and commuted to visit my family whenever I could. After all the changes and separations, I spent as much time as I possibly could with my family, perhaps to make up for all the time my duties kept me from Nga's side.

Living during war time, I came to cherish life even more. From the backline support for the military, I could feel the heat of conflict, which every day became more unmanageable. I learned from reading newspapers and watching television that American soldiers were confronted by war opponents every day. It was a difficult time, not only for me and my family, but for thousands of other Vietnamese families and for American soldiers who were in Vietnam with us and returning home to a hostile nation.

In addition to living with war, we were living in a time when patriotism was not popular. More than once, I had to remind myself I was doing this for a good cause, as good as my brothers had fought and died for. I can still remember the famous quotation from President Kennedy: *"Ask not what your country can do for you — ask what you can do for your country."*

I did not ask what South Vietnam could do for me and my family. I just did what I could to support South Vietnam. It was my beloved country.

## CHAPTER 10

# Mom: My Saddest Time — the Tet Offensive

Most Americans know of Tet only in relation to the Tet Offensive. That is like knowing of Christmas only in relation to a Christmas massacre.

Tet, the Lunar New Year, was the season of celebrations. Families from each region of Vietnam — Northern, Central, and Southern — celebrated with their own distinctive dishes, different styles of home decorations, and customized programs to illustrate the specialties of the regions. Culturally rich, the colorful Tet activities involved large groups of people of all classes, from farmers to businessmen to educators.

Traditionally during Tet, Vietnamese families presented their best dishes to their ancestors. Often they started the preparations weeks ahead of time. Although the children were supposed to go to bed early on the Lunar New Year Eve, parents frequently stayed up all night to prepare the ceremony in remembrance of their ancestors and to pray for their families.

Tet might be considered the Vietnamese equivalent to the American Christmas and New Year. Children were excited to wear their best outfits on the New Year Day. They were even more excited if they received the red envelope with lucky money in it. Tet was the most important occasion for fun. Kids were filled with excitement — often so much they couldn't sleep — but they were also cautioned not to misbehave. According to tradition, good behavior with proper manners during Tet brought good luck for the New Year.

Preparations for Tet could be typically described as two activities: cooking and decorating. On the twenty-ninth day before the New Year Eve, our family cooked Banh Chung and made Mut. Then we decorated our house with Hoa Mai.

Banh Chung is the Tet cake, wrapped in banana leaves, with a rich flavor from steamed sweet rice. It contains pork and green beans in the middle and requires up to eight hours of cooking time, depending on the thickness of the cake. Mut is a special kind of jam or dried fruit, a source of sweet the Vietnamese people love. Making Mut can take hours and hours, depending on the kind of fruit chosen — pineapples, tomatoes, coconuts, jack fruit, and other varieties can be used.

In the South during Tet season, people love to decorate their homes with Hoa Mai, a yellow flower similar to peach flowers but smaller in size. Hoa Mai, which symbolizes prosperity and well-being for the family, often blooms in the warmer weather of the South. The value of a Hoa Mai blossom is determined by the number of petals — the more petals, the more expensive the flower.

While the Southern Vietnamese use Hoa Mai as a symbol of a prosperous New Year, the Northern Vietnamese display Hoa Dao, a red or pink peach flower, during Tet as a symbol to protect themselves against evil or bad luck. People from Hue, in the Central region of Vietnam, celebrated Tet more like the South with Hoa Mai though Hue culture was more enriched because Hue was the Kingdom of Vietnam until 1945.

All of us who were born and grew up in Hue were used to the custom of gathering during Tet. Hue was a peaceful and poetic place, a place with more than a thousand years of traditions. We were proud of Hue because of its many noble features, including the national institute Quoc Hoc, traditional palaces, romantic gardens, the Perfume River Walk, Ngu Mountain, and famous foods. Visitors or tourists who came to Hue often enjoyed Bun Bo and Banh Beo, two of many delicious Hue dishes famous in the Central region. In my memories, Hue was the most charming area of the Central region — a place of literature and art known for distinguished local females, respectable ladies with beautiful accents, soft voices, and polite manners.

I miss Hue with its poetic atmosphere, and I was saddened to see it destroyed and corrupted by the Tet Offensive and the Vietnam War. For such a long time, Hue epitomized a noble Vietnam that had been through many hardships. Hue was a quiet sufferer with tremendous inner beauty. It represented a Vietnam that was wise and shy, but also strong and courageous. I miss Hue, not only because of its lost beauty, but also because of its eternal elegance despite its suffering during wars and political chaos.

### 

New Year Day on the Lunar Year, the Year of the Monkey, 1968. We started the day by presenting our wishes to each other. Wife and husband exchanged wishes; children presented their wishes to the parents and to their siblings. We then prayed in front of the ancestor worship table and prepared for the wishing tour to our close relatives and family members.

We had two children at the time — our oldest daughter Ngoc was one and a half years old, and our second child and oldest son Phuc was six months old. My mother-in-law and the wife of my husband's brother Tho with her four children were staying with us at the time.

Everything seemed normal that holiday until my husband received an order to be at the camp on New Year night. He was directed to stay at headquarters, Su Doan I Bo Binh, or the First Infantry Division, which was stationed in Mang Ca, about two kilometers from where we lived. The headquarters were separated from our hometown by the Trang Tien Bridge, a historical and famous bridge with *6 vai 12 nhip*, or six shoulders and twelve steps, about 400 meters in length. Although it was unusual for Dinh to be at the camp late in the evening on the first New Year Day, I hoped he would come back home on the second New Year Day to continue celebrating Tet.

We were completely unprepared for what happened. I wish we'd had phones or other telecommunications like we have now in the United States. It was 11:00 AM, and I was expecting my husband to go with me to other relatives' houses to wish them the best for the New Year. Instead of my husband, a group of about twenty people carrying guns and wearing black uniforms, rubber sandals, and cone-shape hats pounded on our front door. They were Vietcong, VCs for short, the Vietnamese communists. Only a few of the Vietcong looked older than twenty but every one of them looked mean, aggressive, and intimidating despite their small physical size. They ordered all of my family members to stand in line and started questioning each of us about our relationship to the South Vietnamese government.

After searching every corner of the house, the one that seemed to be the leader barked, "Where did all the men go during Tet?"

They started with my sister-in-law. I don't remember what she answered, but I remember clearly that one guy pointed a gun at me and forced me to answer their questions. They knew my husband was a South Vietnamese officer and wanted to arrest him immediately. They demanded I tell them where he was.

I was shaking in horror and fear. In heavy tones, they threatened to kill everyone at home if they found my husband in the house.

"H-h-he's n-n-not h-h-here," I stammered. I tried to tell them that my husband was seldom at home. Looking at the weapons around their shoulders, listening to the shots they fired randomly through the ceiling, I started crying.

They purposely shot up the ceiling suspecting — probably hoping — my husband was hidden there, then some of them climbed through the ceiling to search for him. They couldn't believe my husband was not home during Tet. They found several of his military uniforms. Tossing these uniforms to me, they ordered me to destroy them right away because the uniforms were the products of *My Nguy*, a noun they used to refer to my husband and the South Vietnamese officers, meaning "American-and-Untruth-Vietnamese people." We still aren't sure what this means. Upset at not being able to find my husband, they shot up and down randomly, cursed at everyone, and then slowly took off. We were all in a state of panic. I broke down, worrying about my husband and wondering if he was safe.

Looking out the window, I saw this group of Vietnamese communists start their search across the street in my neighbor's house. My eyes filled with tears as I watched my neighbor, a low-ranking officer in the South Vietnamese Army, being taken away. He was like a local police officer who didn't get involved with politics. His daily duties were to keep the local area safe from robbery or thefts. I'll never forget the image of my neighbor being captured by those brainwashed VC, hand-cuffed, and forced from his home at gunpoint. A couple of days later, his body was seen not far away from his home.

The VC had killed him, leaving behind his wife with several innocent children.

During Tet, the market was usually open on the second day after the New Year Day since everyone needed fresh food daily. At the time, not many families had refrigerators, and we didn't keep foods for months like we do in the United States. We often cooked more during Tet since dried food was not popular in Vietnam. We loved fresh food and planned to buy it daily, so we were unprepared for a disaster like the Tet Offensive. The markets were shut down, and we had nothing to eat in the following days.

And we couldn't get any sleep, either. We went to the basement temporarily to avoid gunshots and bomb fragments. Commonly, each house had a basement about twenty square feet built with sand and wood during the war. We were in our basement several times a day for about a week. Every night, each time I heard the guns and land mine explosions, I had to wake my children and the rest of the family and rush them all to the basement. Sometimes, only my terror overcame my exhaustion as I carried two babies up and down the steps over and over again.

Noon time. Another rush to the basement — it seemed the drills would never end. Fear tied us together. Eleven of us — my mother-in-law, my sister-in-law and her four children, me and my two little children, and the two helpers — were jammed inside the basement. The rockets poured around our neighborhood. One rocket landed right next to our basement. Sand covered us. Sand covered the exit door. There was no light inside the basement. We had no way out.

I sat right at the door with my little boy in my arms. I felt the sand in my mouth. The basement had collapsed. My baby was sputtering — probably because the sand covered his mouth. I tried to move my arms, to kick my legs outward to escape from the mountain of sand on top of me.

I wouldn't let myself cry but forced myself to focus on moving my arms to get my baby out of the door. Finally! I saw sunlight outside the basement. I got out first with my son in my arms. I scraped the sand from his face, nose, and his body to help him breathe better. As soon as I realized he was alive and safe, I started crying.

Then I turned my focus to my daughter Ngoc, who was being held by a helper. When I couldn't see her, I screamed.

My cries were answered by Lanh, my husband's loyal subordinate, who rushed from the back shed. We pulled everyone, including my daughter, to safety.

We were lucky to have Lanh around during the Tet Offensive. From time to time, my husband assigned him to help me with my kids while he was on duty. Lanh was an interesting character, and I believe Buddha blessed us by bringing him to be my husband's subordinate and also his driver. Lanh believed in the circle of life — he said everyone has his or her own time; if the time comes, one will die, sooner or later.

Lanh's attitude made him a brave person. During the Tet Offensive, he never went to the basement; he said there was no point in worrying about rockets, if his time came, he would be happy to go. I spoke with Lanh for the last time when I had to leave Vietnam to come to America. His bravery and attitude helped us all through those difficult days.

Even with Lanh's help, however, we lost our confidence and spirit. I missed my husband and worried about him all the time.

My house was located near Ben Ngu, a river walk straight to Phu Cam Church. After the rocket destroyed our basement, we couldn't stay at home any longer. With my mother-in-law's determination and with Lanh's help, hand-in-hand together we walked to Phu Cam Church. During the walk, rockets dropped along the river. Some rockets dropped deep down in the water, which shot up as a big fountain all around — in front of us, behind us, to our left and right. We prayed as we walked. Occasionally, we had to lie down to avoid fragments. Suddenly I realized life and death are just a hair's distance apart.

I saw American bodies here and there. There had been a battle between the VC and the Americans who were with the South Vietnamese officers. Lots of bodies lay along the river walk. I dared not look. Blindly, I walked with my son in my arms and my mother-in-law beside me. The helper still held my daughter, who was crying and confused by the rockets' sounds. Bullets fell like a summer rain ... here and there, unpredictable.

We finally arrived at the Phu Cam Church, which was filled with people. We all hoped the VC would leave the church alone because according to Vietnamese tradition, churches and pagodas are spiritual places not to be violated. We hoped if the VC were Vietnamese, they would at least honor the basic foundation of tradition respecting churches and pagodas and would not harm us in these spiritual places. But ... the shooting started again, very near us.

Churches and pagodas were no longer peaceful places in Vietnam! My mother-in-law believed that there were VC among the people at the church. Her instinct and concerns made us worry that more dangerous times were to come. We soon left the church by the back door, walking away without any particular direction. Beside the small road, we saw the Linh Quang Pagoda.

Starving and tired from the long walk, we stopped at the pagoda. Rockets and gunfire still poured around us. I don't know how we had made it as far as we did. Small rockets, gunshots, and mines exploded and dropped to the ground, creating millions of fragments like huge fireworks.

The pagoda's peaceful view became a war zone — smoke and fires, dust and sand, total chaos. My heart beat faster as the thought that we could be killed any second raced through my mind over and over again. As I looked at my two little babies and my other family members who hadn't had enough to eat for over ten days, I prayed.

I prayed the rockets would not hit us. I prayed the pagoda would protect us with its miracle wall. I prayed the lives of my children and my husband would be spared. And, I prayed I would see my husband again.

More than ever, I missed my husband. I felt the whole world weighing down my little shoulders. All I could do was pray.

The 15th of January, Lunar Year, 5:00 PM. My family without my husband was still at the Linh Quang Pagoda. Random rockets hit the ground. The sounds grew louder and louder every time a rocket hit the road or the yard in front of us. I was holding my six-month-old son. My little daughter slept in the helper's arms. As we prayed, I felt a pain in my leg.

### 

The next thing I knew, I woke from unconsciousness. A rocket had hit the roof of Linh Quang Pagoda right over our heads. When I came to and looked around, I saw dead bodies and wounded people. The sight was too terrible to be real — I thought that I was having a horrific nightmare. Then I looked down to see blood covering my son and myself. I couldn't move the lower half of my body.

Probably because of losing so much blood, I passed out again. I don't know how long I lay there unconscious, but it must have been several hours. When I once again came to I saw all the blood and realized my baby wasn't moving. I almost panicked before I realized that my little son's heart was still beating.

I prayed as I felt his body with my hand. He had lost his

pinky toe and his breathing was weak — but he was breathing! There was so much blood it was hard to tell its source, but I realized much of it had come from his stomach, probably from the rocket's fragments. And he was unconscious. I prayed for him through sobs and tears. He was my hope — he had to live.

I couldn't locate the other members of my family. They'd probably run to avoid the rocket. We'd planned ahead — if a rocket came, we would all run, then try to find each other later. I had to believe in the fortune of life. Maybe Lanh was right. When one's time comes, maybe no one could help — all I could do was pray.

"Does the baby need help?" I heard the woman's comforting voice, but the glare blocked her face.

"He's hurt. He's very hurt, but I don't know how bad."

"Here. Give him to me." She reached down. "I'll get help for him."

I almost handed him to her, then my body turned cold. I cradled him more tightly. I could not turn loose of my child, my hope.

"No," I whispered. Then I spoke louder. "No. My family will find us soon. They will get help for us."

She finally walked away. I feared I had given up my son's chance of survival, but I knew my family would not survive without him.

I dared not look around. If I looked at the dead bodies I might recognize one of my loved ones, and I didn't think I could hold myself together if that happened. I worried so much about my daughter. Where was she?

Hopelessness and despair stabbed my heart and soul. I wondered what would happen if my time came. How could my babies survive without me? Then, I heard a sound, a little sound, a tiny sound. Oh my goodness — my daughter! Her steps were not strong yet, but she walked ... she walked over the dead bodies to find me! I reached out and tried to stand up to hold her, but I could not stand.

"Please, come here with me, baby," I whispered. Buddha had granted me miracle strength. I had to live! I thanked Buddha for protecting me and both my children. My daughter saw me. She walked faster and faster toward me, naive enough to ignore the dead bodies she stepped on. I cried and reached out to take her in my arms. I hugged her tightly to my chest, crying and praying. I searched her body, touching her feet, her hands, and her face. Thank goodness, she was perfect! I forgot my wounded leg. I forgot the pains from fragments that had stabbed so viciously just a second ago. Seeing my daughter alive and safe with my little boy, though still unconscious, resting beside my right leg, erased my pains and turned my tears of hurt and fear into tears of joy and thanksgiving.

An hour later, when I heard no more rockets, my mind calmed a bit. I looked around for my relatives and loved ones. Where was my mother-in-law? Where were the helpers? Later, I was told that, after she saw the rocket hit the roof, my helper took my daughter and ran out of the pagoda with the others. The helper was too panicked and worried about her own life to pay attention to my daughter. She ran so fast she lost the little girl somewhere on the inside road, about one hundred meters away from where I was wounded, but she continued running for her life. I didn't blame the helper for not taking care of my daughter. I don't know how my daughter found me — it had to be a miracle for us to be reunited in the middle of all the chaos, and this miracle certainly helped us in the dark days that followed.

I'm not sure what happened next. Order had not been re-established, and traffic was still stopped because of destroyed roadways and lack of communication. The VC were in control of the side of the river where I was hidden with the monks and my neighbors while my husband was on the other side of the river. We didn't know for sure which area belonged to what side anymore. There were no more rocket sounds, but random gunshots still caused chaos and fear.

People started looking for their families. I was fortunate because my next door neighbor and his two sons had also come to the Linh Quang Pagoda to avoid the rockets. They found us and helped us. The neighbor, who had a medical education background, guarded me carefully, dosing me with a couple of drops of water at the time. He said if I drank more water, I would die from losing more blood. The neighbor asked his sons to take turns watching me all night. He also took care of my children and asked other people to look for my missing family members.

The next day, my neighbor and the monks at the Linh Quang Pagoda made a bed out of cloth to transport me to the Central Hospital, about three kilometers away from the pagoda. Sometimes the group had to stop to avoid communist attacks. Occasionally, I heard the voices of communists ordering us to halt at their checkpoints. One time, we were confronted by a group of about a dozen communists with guns. They shouted at us and demanded the group stop immediately.

When they came closer to search us, they found me injured in the cotton bed, surrounded by monks in *ao ca sa mau lam*, a type of gray monks' uniform. The fifteen- to twenty-year-old monks begged the communists to let us go. They told the VC I was too weak to stay, and they needed to take me to the Su Nu Pagoda, a small pagoda between the Linh Quang and Central Hospital. The communists looked at me, with a purple lip, lying in the cotton bed and finally let us go.

We arrived at the Su Nu Pagoda at about 2:00 PM. The shooting continued; our lives were still in danger. At the Su Nu Pagoda, I felt an incredible thirst. Then I saw a large ceramic water container, a kind of countryside container the Vietnamese called *Lu nuoc*. I was so thirsty I could imagine myself drinking all of the water, about fifty gallons! I cried for some water! The monks told me it would be bad if they let me drink freely and gave the same reason my neighbor had — I would lose more blood if I drank much water. One monk put a couple drops of water on my lips to ease my thirst. I then passed into unconsciousness again ...

When I woke up, I saw my mother sitting next to me at the Su Nu Pagoda. She was too excited and happy to act normally. I saw her turn to the monks.

"Please," she begged. "Take her to the Central Hospital to treat her injured leg. You can see how much blood she and my grandson are both losing. I'm afraid they'll die if they don't get professional medical attention right away."

The monks talked among themselves a little bit.

Thinking she wasn't getting through to them, my mother reminded them, "I've been here a day and two nights — ever since I learned my daughter was hurt in the rocket attack. I've tried and tried to wake her up, but this is the first time she's responded. I thought I was going to lose her every time her lips and body turned purple. Her breathing got so weak it was hard to be sure she was really still breathing. I even wondered if she had any blood or if her blood circulation had stopped for a while." My mother took a deep breath and looked at the monks. "There's hope for her now if you'll just get her to the hospital."

The monks looked at each other and agreed to take me to the Central Hospital. Four monks carried me on the cloth bed. I was so fortunate to have great friends, neighbors, and monks to save my life! I was even more fortunate to have my brave and loving mother that I loved so much.

The first people to leave the Su Nu Pagoda were the monks who carried me on the cloth bed. Following us were a couple more groups, each several hundred meters apart; the last group included my mother holding my injured son in her arms. We all headed to the Central Hospital. Later, I learned that while my mother walked with the monks with my son in her arms, the Vietnamese communists ordered her to stop. She ignored them. The VC shouted that if she continued to move, they would shoot her.

My mother answered, "I don't care what you say or what you threaten — all I care about is this baby's life. He needs medical attention as soon as possible."

Closing her eyes, my mother just kept walking without stopping to consider the consequences. She risked her life to save my son! Fortunately, the communists just shot up the air to threaten her. My mother's courage saved my son's life.

My son had many scars on his body after the rocket attack during the Tet Offensive. Thank goodness, he was still young, too little to remember the pain of his wounds, but his missing toe will always remind him of the war. This event created a strong connection — far more than simple closeness — among the three of us — my mother, my son, and me. I am blessed to have such a loving family.

As tragic as the Tet Offensive was, the sadness and sorrow did not stop there. Later days in Vietnam brought more suffering that I will never forget ...

## CHAPTER 11

# Dad: Living the War as a Soldier

I vividly remember my days in Hue during the Tet Offensive when the North violated the cease fire agreement and attacked the South. Communists controlled Hue for almost a month until the American and South Vietnamese armies liberated the area. From the day I was called to report to the camp on the first night of Tet, life in Vietnam became extremely difficult for all of us.

It was Tet of 1968. I left home around 7:00 PM on the New Year Day and got to the camp around 7:30 PM. At the camp, we were divided into squads to act as security guards around the inner city of Hue. Five or six gates in the circle walls separated the inner side, or Noi Thanh, and outer side, or Ngoai Thanh, of Hue City.

The infantry officers were responsible for the security of these gates to prevent a Vietcong attack inside Hue City. I was on the back-up lists. Some officers didn't make it to the camp; perhaps they didn't hear the commands on the radio or didn't receive the telegrams. Later I learned many of those officers who didn't report to camp on time were caught in their own homes and executed by the Vietcong. I was lucky to be on duty during Tet!

On the radio, civilians were warned to be inside at night, while military personnel had to be on guard 24/7. I thought this was a temporary command and hoped I could be home soon to take my family out for the Tet observance. I severely underestimated what would happen during the coming days, and I couldn't contact Nga. The communists' attack was too fast for us to mount a response. Like many other officers on guard, I ran for my life without any way to get in touch with my family.

There were ten or twelve soldiers in a squad led by one officer, a captain or first lieutenant. I led a squad to An Hoa Gate, assigned a role to each member of the team, then went back to camp to get ready for the next shift. When I returned with the new squad for the second shift, we heard some gunshots above our heads. At first, I thought it was random shots from nervous guards, but then I saw many people running on the wall, most wearing black uniforms and carrying big guns. One guard screamed, "It's VC; it's VC." A series of gunshots was aimed toward that guard. I knew then the Vietcong had attacked us.

After I assigned a duty to each person on the team, we realized we weren't equipped to fight back. We couldn't confront the Vietcong on the walls or from the unprotected corners. We finally separated the squad to withdraw from the area and agreed to meet at headquarters as soon as we could.

On the road, I could see Vietcong were already in control and searching for soldiers like us. Taking a deep breath, I knocked on the door of a nearby house and put my life in the hands of the man who opened the door. I introduced myself to a gentleman around my age and told him I was seeking refuge from the Vietcong. He opened the door and took me in. I forgot what the owner's name was, but he told me he was a student attending a college in Quy Nhon, majoring in education. He advised me to discard my military uniform and offered me civilian clothes to hide my identity from the Vietcong. I asked the owner if he could give me his spare student identification so I could have proof of being a civilian. I hoped the Vietcong would give me a break if they thought I was just a student. I couldn't afford to disclose my identity to them — they could have executed me immediately. With borrowed clothes and false identification, I left the house and searched for a way out. I got lost in a strange area where I had never been before, a huge field with dirt roads around it.

Confused by several circle walks, I decided to wait until morning, hoping with light I could see everything around me better. My body ached, and I was very hungry. I was tired but couldn't afford to sleep. Every fiber of my being braced for the possibility of a face-to-face meeting with the Vietcong. I hoped that didn't happen though the threat hung over me like a black cloud.

I wondered if Nga knew the Vietcong were in control, and if she knew I was hiding. I didn't know what would happen to my wife and babies if the Vietcong searched the house and if they knew I was an officer. I told myself to be more optimistic, and it was my family that gave me the hope. I breathed a prayer each time I thought of my family.

I needed to get out of the strange area and report to my unit. I walked and walked until I passed a field. Then at the end of the road, I learned I was in Tay Loc, a small village far from the Northwest area. I finally knew where I was, but I still could not contact headquarters or my family.

In Tay Loc, I ran into First Sergeant D's wife. D was my friend in the unit. His family asked me if I had seen him since the day before, but I didn't have any news about him. I told them I was on the run and I was very tired. I accepted their invitation to stay with them until I could gain back my energy. D's wife and children kept me safe in their home and fed me well. They had arranged a day bed in the living room, which was the first room from the main entrance, and reminded me to get plenty of sleep to prepare me to return to the unit. I was lucky to receive help from my friends and their families. Buddha blessed me and my family during these difficult years. Many of my friends and subordinates were there for me when I needed help.

Tired from the run, I fell asleep on the day bed. I was awakened by a tap on my shoulder. A fully-armed Vietcong stood in front of me. I thought to myself, "This is the end!"

The Vietcong ordered me to follow him outside. He demanded to see my identification. Shaking, I pulled out the false identification and handed it to him. There was another group of Vietcong next to me, asking other people to show their identification as well. The picture on my identification card did not match my description, but somehow the Vietcong did not notice.

Nearby, I recognized one of the guards from the second squad team in An Hoa two nights before; he was being arrested. Apparently he didn't have false identification as I did. His hands were roped tightly while the Vietcong pulled him away. I felt helpless but lucky that the brave young man gave no indication he recognized me. I was consumed by a powerful guilt even with the realization any attempt to save him would doom me as well. Still reeling from my emotions, I thanked Buddha the Vietcong didn't give me a hard time or question me about my identification card. If there was any suspicion, I would probably have been taken away and executed.

After reviewing my identification, the man handed me a stack of *Truyen Don* or propagated document and asked me to hand these flyers out to everyone I saw on the road. I kept the *Truyen Don* with me as my passport to continue my walk back to the unit. I decided if I ran into other Vietcong troops, I would show the propaganda flyers as proof of my willingness to obey their request. This tactic served me well until I found my way to my friend, a South Vietnam higher-ranking officer, N.

When I arrived at N's house, he was happy to see me but warned me he had to hide in the ceiling to avoid the Vietcong. There were many signs of the Vietcong nearby, so N's wife protected us by supplying us with food and water on the roof. N hadn't been out of the house for the two days. For the next couple of days, we watched the fully-armed Vietcong marching outside the house. Luckily for us, they hadn't started searching yet. We couldn't risk a search, so we planned our escape.

N's wife provided us with water and dried food, and she checked the surroundings before we left the house. The gunshots were random. We waited until large groups of people were leaving the area to escape the head-on fighting between the Vietcong and the South Army. After saying goodbye to N's wife, we joined the crowd and made our way back to the First Division.

We found the road leading to the First Division blocked by a major conflict. We decided to separate; N went to his mother-in-law's, and I spent two days with my grandmother waiting for further news. It was hard to know who was in control because I could see both Marines and Vietcong in the area. Several times a day, Vietcong with guns walked around the neighborhood — right behind my grandmother's backyard.

Then I heard the Marine troops. I was thrilled to recognize the South Vietnamese Marine uniforms. I learned they had re-gained control of the area and planned to take back Hue from the Vietcong. I said goodbye to my grandmother and my aunts and reported to the Marine commander as an officer on the run from the Vietcong. He contacted the Mang Ca chief officer, who was happy to know I was safe with the Marines. It took me more than five days to get back to my unit, where I was greeted by the chief officer, then given three days to rest.

I still couldn't contact home. I wish we'd had telephone lines then as we do now. After learning the Vietcong had attacked Hue, I feared Nga and my family were under their control as well. I couldn't drive back home because the Trang Tien Bridge had been bombed by the communists. The South Vietnamese Army controlled the northwest side of the Perfume River, or the Ta Ngan area, while the Vietcong controlled the opposite side of the Perfume River, or Huu Ngan area. I was in Ta Ngan while Nga was in Huu Ngan.

## CHAPTER 12

# Mom: The Aftermath of Tet

In the middle of the chaos of the Tet Offensive, my parents came to the Linh Quang Pagoda to avoid the rockets. My father was among the many people killed after several Vietcong attacked the Linh Quang Pagoda. I received the news of his death when I was in the Central Hospital. With my son and me both injured, the bad news seemed like tropical rain beating down on us. In a couple of weeks, I had lost many of my loved ones to the Vietcong.

I admired my father very much; he was an inspiration to me. Not only was he a loving father, but he was also my teacher. He taught me the values of a traditional Vietnamese lady — to be polite, thoughtful, and respectful. He taught me how to be patient with life.

He reminded me life could sometimes appear unfair for many people, but with hard work and patience, they could overcome the hardships. My father told me, "Life is a mirror; if you smile at it, you will see you smile. If you cry in front of it, you will see you cry."

Until recently, every time I made a mistake, I thought of the image of my father looking at me, explaining why I should learn to improve myself. Each time I lost my temper, I heard my father reminding me to use my words carefully and to be more patient with others.

I have learned to be patient with life, but I also believe life was very unfair to my father, who was a great man. I never saw him lose his temper. He earned the respect of others in the neighborhood — not because we were rich, but because he was so polite and such a gentleman.

He died when he was sixty years old. He worked hard all his life to raise our family, and he never truly had an opportunity to relax and enjoy the fruits of his labors. Sometimes I wish I'd had more time with him, to give back just a tiny fraction of what he gave to me, to say thank you to him for all the energy and emotional support he gave to us: me, my siblings, and my mother.

I still miss my father very much. I miss him so much that it hurts each time I think of him. I rarely use the word hate to refer to other human beings, but I hated the Vietcong for taking my father's life. Buddha has taught me to forgive and to be humble. Nothing I can do will ever change the brutal fact my father is no longer with us. Only in our memories does he live. Through the years, I have learned to forgive because that was the best way to ease the spirit of my mind, but I cannot forget. I cannot forget what the Vietcong did to my family, my friends, my relatives, and to Hue.

I remember Uncle Hai, my aunt's husband. They lived in a comfortable house in Huong-Thuy, a small village close to Hue. Uncle Hai, who was very educated, was a bookkeeper for the local government agency. Most people in the village knew him by name, both because he was a master of the village's knowledge, and also because he was always willing to help others.

On the day the Vietcong attacked Hue, they also occupied Huong-Thuy. My aunt told us the first thing the communists did when they were in control was search for the local government employees. Uncle Hai, one of many, was arrested at his own house. My aunt told us the communists used *day thung*, a custom-made big coconut string, to lock Uncle Hai's arms behind his back before linking him in a human chain with the other prisoners. These people were dragged away from the village. Then, the communists ordered that no one could follow Uncle Hai and the others who were all involved with the South Vietnam government, and it was very important that they were punished and made examples.

Months after the Vietcong occupations in Hue, several mass graves were discovered and bodies were recovered from under mud and sand. Local people who lived around these mass graves stated that what happened had been too horrible to believe. Before rushing these innocent people to the graves to be murdered, the Vietcong declared they had owed the communist party and the Vietnamese people a debt that could only be repaid by their own blood.

To me, more than just a hard worker, Uncle Hai was a good Vietnamese person willing to reach out as much as he could to help others. Months after the New Year began when order was reestablished in Huong-Thuy after the Tet Offensive, my aunt received the bad news. Uncle Hai, among many innocent Hue people, was murdered; he suffered the pain of starvation for days before being buried alive.

My aunt later told me that Uncle Hai's body was recovered — piece by piece. He was identified first by the plastic identification card in his pocket, and then last, by the wedding ring on his finger. I remember my aunt's face when she told me about Uncle Hai. I cannot describe how sad she looked. Tears welled up in her empty eyes, but she was too hurt to cry out loud. When Uncle Hai died, he left behind my aunt with several blameless children.

Similar tragedies happened to my neighbors and my other

relatives. One of my neighbors Ba' worked in the local government agency. He was a warrant officer with the lowest military ranking. Ba' and his wife had two handsome sons about fifteen and seventeen years old, still high-school students. On the sixteenth day after the New Year, Ba's two sons were taken away by the Vietcong, searched, and buried alive. Afterwards, Mr. and Mrs. Ba' both suffered severe mental breakdowns.

The neighbor who lived across the street from my home was arrested and killed by a shot to the front of his head. His family, a housewife and four children, found his body not far from their home.

Each time the Vietcong occupied a town or village near Hue, all the men of military age were arrested to be "analyzed" and "judged" whether their names appeared on the communists' "black lists" or not. Many were shot to death; others were tortured and their bodies dragged to the train tracks. While some were buried alive, others simply disappeared. In most cases, no one knew anything about their men once the Vietcong took them. These tragedies did not happen only to men, but also to housewives and children, even to many young women in the brightest time of their lives.

I called my brother-in-law's sister Tuyet my older sister, because she was such a sweetheart and I respected her. She was a typical lady of Hue, with both the inside and outside appearance of a *noble Hue*. I don't believe that Tuyet could hurt have anyone, not even a tiny ant, but she was also buried alive by the communists. Her body was found in a mass murder site similar to Uncle Hai's case.

Local people told me the Vietcong did not like the quality of life Tuyet had. In general, these Vietcong believed wealthy, beautiful, and educated people were evil. The communists attributed her appearance of a better economic status to the "exploitation" of Vietnam by her brother. Several days before the New Year, Tuyet's brother had come to visit her and his mother in his South Vietnamese police officer's uniform. People suspected her younger brother's visit caused Tuyet to be buried alive!

How could someone be sentenced to death just because she appeared to be wealthier and prettier than others? Why couldn't the communists stay in the North and respect the Geneva Agreement? Why did they cause so much pain for Hue, for my relatives, for my family, and for me?

I learned of all these deaths and tragedies as I lay wounded in Central Hospital. This knowledge overwhelmed me with despair and helplessness. Each time I received bad news, I felt a terrible pain in my heart. I was exhausted, both mentally and physically. Covering my face with the hospital's pillow, I closed my eyes to rest, but my mind would not shut down.

Every time I woke, I felt the terrible pain and remembered clearly what had happened to my leg. Because I had lost so much blood, my body was very weak, and I had a severe headache. From the knee to the ankle, my injured leg was swollen to triple the size of my normal leg. Because it took so long for me to get medical attention, my leg had become seriously infected.

There was no chief doctor at Central Hospital at the time. Most of the doctors were running for their lives or had been captured by the communists. There was a shortage of antibiotic medicine — the supply of medicine was limited because of traffic delays and the large number of patients. I was in emergency intensive care because I had lost so much blood, and no doctor would make an official decision about treating me. The pain and despair threatened to defeat my weakened body and spirit.

Lying in a tiny and dirty hospital bed, I often wanted to give up. Then I finally spoke with my mother. She did a great job of calming me and bringing me back to the reality that I had to face. I listened to the voice of my daughter, and I could see the discomfort of my little son who had lost his toe at this early age. With my mother's encouragement, I pulled myself together.

People who came to visit their families at Central Hospital told me about the recovery of Hue, town by town, village by village, but the communication wasn't much improved yet. I worried about my husband's safety and asked other people in the hospital for help contacting him. I could hear radio broadcasts three times a day. I asked my next-door neighbor to place ads on the radio to inform my husband about our situation.

Dinh received the news and tried his best to come to Central Hospital for me. The South Army had gained control back in Hue, but the road conditions were still dangerous for traveling, especially between the two sides of the Perfume River. Dinh asked for help from his army headquarters. The headquarters' personnel escorted Dinh with several other South Vietnamese officers in similar situations by helicopter directly to Central Hospital. We were finally reunited about three weeks after I was injured.

## CHAPTER 13

# Dad: Reunited with My Family

Two weeks after the Tet Offensive, one of the officers told me he'd heard on the radio that Nga was severely injured during a communist attack. My whole world almost collapsed when I heard the news. I didn't know how to get to the other side of the river. With lots of fighting still raging, ground transportation was dangerous. When I learned that Nga and Phuc were in Central Hospital, I walked to the headquarters office and asked for help to visit my family on the other side.

The headquarters administrative assistant accepted my request and let me ride along on a helicopter to Central Hospital, but there was no place to land at the hospital. We landed at a school stadium about a mile away, a long walk through an area badly damaged by the conflicts.

Running into the hospital, I could see from afar that Nga was crying. Her leg, especially the knee, was burning red. My mother-in-law held my son Phuc, his foot wrapped with white cloth and tape. Tears came to my eyes when I learned how much Nga had been through, and my heart broke when I was told of my father-in-law's death. I didn't see Ngoc; my mother had been taking care of her at home since the South gained back control. My mother-in-law did double-duty: taking care of Nga and feeding Phuc at the hospital. With three days off, I stayed at the hospital to take care of Nga. My mother and mother-in-law took turns bringing Ngoc and Phuc to visit us.

### 

The years following the Tet Offensive created many mixed feelings for me. I struggled to face the reality of Nga's injury. I tried my very best to help her with her damaged self-esteem and to regain our normal life, but it was very tough. Perpetually on the run, we were constantly separated; I had my military duties, and Nga had to take care of the children. Hope for a simple peaceful life evaporated — it seemed an impossible dream.

## CHAPTER 14

# Mom: The Pain of Loss and the Happiness of Recovery

I was so happy! I was happy because my husband was safe and healthy. I was happy because my concerns were divided by half. I was happy because my children and their father were reunited. I was happy because my husband was protecting me and my children.

Even with the nurses' help and my husband's care, my leg continued to worsen.

A mature nurse named Mrs. Cuc gave Dinh some advice. "Your wife will have a hard time getting better if she stays here at Central Hospital. We're overloaded here, and we don't have professional doctors or sufficient medicine and equipment. You need to ask for help at an American hospital. With your military background, you can ask for a passport to be accepted."

With Mrs. Cuc's recommendation, Dinh contacted the Nguyen Tri Phuong Hospital, a military facility located within the Mang Ca First Infantry Division. Because my husband was a South Vietnamese Officer, he received the passport for family care. It took him a day to get me admitted to the Nguyen Tri Phuong Hospital.

My mother stayed at Central Hospital to take care of my little son. Though he had lost a toe and had many scratches, his health improved daily. My mother had to feed him from the bottle since I could no longer breast feed him.

For the first time during this run from the Vietcong, I slept in a decent bed. The next morning, two doctors and a nurse came to examine me.

After the examination, the first doctor introduced himself as Dr. Lac. "Ma'am, your leg has been badly injured and now is badly infected. The best thing to do is to amputate the leg to avoid further serious infections that could be fatal."

"No!" I couldn't believe my ears. I began to cry.

"Can't you save the leg, Doctor?" Dinh asked.

The second doctor spoke. "We think it's too risky. Your wife is in grave danger. Better to lose a leg than to lose her life."

"I can't lose a leg. I have to take care of my children! Please don't cut my leg off." I begged and cried and begged some more.

Dinh looked as stricken as I felt. "Doctors, she's so young. We have two children — the youngest is just six months old. Our babies need their mother to be able to take care of them. Isn't there something else you can do?"

"I'm strong," I said. "I'm willing to take some risks for whatever other options there are. Please, give me a chance."

Dinh continued to plead, but I began to cry so much I couldn't say any more.

Dr. Lac finally said, "We need to discuss this case again. We'll get back to you with the decision of whether to amputate your leg or not."

Two hours after the initial consultation, Dr. Lac came to

my bed. "In order to minimize the infection, the best I can do is perform surgery. It might take multiple procedures to finish." He looked me in the eye and said, "I want to be sure both of you understand nothing is guaranteed. If this surgery isn't successful, I'll have to amputate the leg to save your life." He paused before he continued. "In fact, because you have such a high fever from the infection, amputating the leg might actually speed up your recovery. So you have to be prepared for an amputation — I'll try to avoid it, but we may have to do it anyway. Is that clear?"

Dinh and I were both too overcome with emotion to speak; all we could do was nod our understanding and agreement.

Dr. Lac then turned to Dinh and said, "You've got a special woman here — she has a strong will to survive."

The doctor ordered the nurse to have the equipment ready for my surgery the following day and left us to wait anxiously for the next morning to arrive ...

At 8:00 AM the next day, Dr. Lac and several nurses moved me to the operating room. My husband waited outside as nervous and worried as I was. Then the nurses gave me anesthesia for the surgery, which lasted about three hours. I was unconscious until 10 PM, but I never found out why it took me so long to wake up.

Every morning, I feared the footsteps of the nurses. Each time they changed the dressing I felt the pain going through my spine. There was a big hole in my knee after the operation. The doctors normally poured medicine and antibiotics in this hole, causing excruciating pain beyond anything I had ever imagined.

For almost a month, each morning I fought my own war with the pain of my injuries and my treatment. And each time I triumphed, I felt the achievement of victory.

On top of the physical pain, however, bad news about the deaths of loved ones drained my strength and taxed my emotional state even further. News of another loss added to the agony in my heart, and finally defeated my patience with life. I felt depressed and hopeless. With the support of my mother and my husband, I tried my best to overcome the hardship and focus on the critical need to fight against the odds and survive.

Even with the hospital care and expertise, my leg was still swollen and the tissues badly bruised. Once again, Dr. Lac decided to put me through an operation. He said the second operation was critical to save my leg. If it wasn't successful, we should be prepared for the amputation.

I don't know all the details of the procedure, but I learned Dr. Lac replaced the infected tissues in my knee and ankle with healthy tissues from the upper part of my leg. At the time, this procedure was very rare in Vietnam. We were lucky to have Dr. Lac.

Dinh told me the operation took Dr. Lac and his assistants more than five hours. When I woke up, I saw my husband standing next to my bed. Somehow I sensed the success of this second operation. Even through the intense pain, I could see the light at the end of my dark tunnel.

I finally observed my situation using my head instead of my wounded heart. Although the random gunshots terrified me and sometimes Dinh had to carry me to the hospital basement to avoid rocket attacks, I was truly very lucky. I was lucky not only to survive, but also to have my loving husband Dinh. Lucky to have my mother and mother-in-law who helped care for me and my children through the ordeal. I was lucky to have friends, monks, and neighbors who cared for me and got me to the hospital through the danger. Lucky to have a nurse who helped us get to the right hospital. And lucky to have doctors and medical staff who provided the care I needed.

For several weeks when my wounded leg and wounded heart were still very fatigued, Dinh took care of me and the children at night in addition to his military duties. As I improved, I saw how hard it was for him since he had almost no sleep. Even so, his love, words, care, and support nourished my spirit like gentle drops of rain nourish the earth. While I spent six months lying in bed in the Nguyen Tri Phuong Hospital, I had lots of time to reminisce about my life and to experience the pain of losing my beloved Hue. Gradually I came to terms with my grief as my loving husband helped me realize life is still beautiful as long as I have my family.

## CHAPTER 15

# Mom: The War Rages On

I lay in the hospital bed for six months, a long time with too much sad news. My husband took care of me, my two children, and my mother-in-law. And he was still responsible for his on-call duties at work. I can't imagine how Dinh managed all that stress and stayed so patient with me.

I'll always remember the terrible pain I suffered when my foot first touched the ground after six months in bed. Even with the support of wooden crutches, I felt like thousands of needles were pricking my leg. My whole body hurt.

Dinh stood at my side encouraging me. "You can do it. Just take one step."

Finally I took the first step, and I felt such a wave of dizziness I feared I might fall. Between the discomfort and the low self-esteem I felt because of my imperfection, I was tempted to give up. But Dinh said, "You're doing good. Please take another step."

The pain was excruciating, and I felt a fresh wave of dizziness with each step. But I kept trying and after several days I could walk on crutches by myself without falling down. Dr. Lac signed the paperwork for me to go home although I would have to be on crutches for weeks.

I was happy and sad at the same time. Happy because I could go home with my husband and see my children. Happy because I could sleep in my own bed, live in my own house, and take care of some family business. However, I was sad because I had become a partially disabled woman.

Although my knee and ankle were healed, I couldn't move my leg or stress it as normal. Life changed for me rapidly when I started walking without crutches. I felt more distance with everyone around me. My self-esteem was still very low. Although no one said anything that made me sad, I could see the differences in people's eyes. Perhaps people around me were sympathizing because I was disabled at such a young age. Perhaps some of them thought I was a heavy burden for my husband. Though people didn't say much, their manners made me very sad, and my husband could see how their behavior affected me.

I didn't want to bother anyone, especially my loved ones, but I began to feel negative about life. In spite of my disability and my negative attitude, though, Dinh continued to give me support and encouragement. He showed his love even more than when we were first married, more than when I was prettier and much healthier. My husband's love nurtured my self-esteem, and I overcame my negative feelings a couple of months later.

I like to remember another famous Vietnamese proverb: *Hoan nan thay chan tinh,* or, "When you confront hardships, it's when you find your true love." I have met my true love in life, my husband Dinh.

During the war, our family constantly moved. After the Tet Offensive, Hue rebuilt, and finally businesses re-opened. We had to start the family business again from the beginning. Since rice was the common trade good in Vietnam, we were doing very well.

In 1970, our daughter Thuy was born. In 1971, I had our son Dzung. Within four years from the Tet Offensive, our family had grown to six members: my husband, me, and the four children. Ngoc was six; Phuc was five; Thuy was two and a half years old, and Dzung was eighteen months old.

In 1972, we went to Quang Tri to visit some friends and relatives. Quang Tri was a city about fifty kilometers north of Hue. It is near the seventeenth parallel, and its north side belonged to the communists. Unfortunately, we were stuck in the Red Summer conflict between the South and the North while we were coming back to Hue from Quang Tri.

I can never forget what I saw on the National Road to Hue. Many people traveled the road to avoid the Vietcong. Children cried. Elders walked tiredly. Military trucks carried soldiers on duty. Then I saw a rocket launched. Memories of the Tet Mau Than, or Year of the Monkey Tet, made my heart beat harder.

Each time a rocket landed on the road, I saw casualties. A baby, just a few months old, sucked its dead mother's breast. The whole scene was like a horror movie! Dead bodies lay everywhere. I was horrified.

But there was no time for me to feel sad or grieve for what I saw. My four little children started feeling sick. Ngoc, Phuc, Thuy, and Dzung all had real bad fevers. Then I saw red dots appearing on the faces and bodies of all of my children. Dinh and I took turns caring for the kids on the run, while the driver was cautioned to move in the flow of the chaos. Exhausted, I fought worry and panic.

Finally we arrived in Hue. We were lucky because our neighbor Dr. Giau, who was known in town for children's medicine, helped us cure them. Dr. Giau gave my children some medicine and showed me how to care for them. Thank goodness all the kids recovered, and my stress level was reduced. Later, we read in the news and heard on the radio the

National Road was named *Dai Lo Kinh Hoang* or "the Horror Avenue" because so many dead bodies were found after the Red Summer conflict.

In Hue, news of the Vietcong's move toward the South made us more nervous. At night, we couldn't go outside, and occasionally we could hear gunshots though far away and random. On the news, people were alerted that the Vietcong could attack Hue again. The region became very chaotic, and many people moved to the South. Dinh rented a car for us to move to DaNang to be with my sister Le and her family, who had moved to DaNang a couple of years after the Tet Offensive. Because of his duties, he couldn't go with us — he had to stay with his unit in Hue.

Without my husband, I led the four children on the road from Hue to DaNang to avoid the Vietcong. My mother and my mother-in-law also joined us on the run.

The National Road Number 1, from Hue to DaNang, was crowded. We had to pass through the Hai Van Hill, which was about twenty kilometers long, one way, and very dangerous. People, traveling by any means they could — bicycles, motorcycles, cars, trucks, even on foot — jammed the small road with no order whatsoever. Our car couldn't move because the road was too crowded. Normally we could travel from Hue to DaNang in only two to three hours. Now, in the chaos of war, it took us a day to get to my sister Le's house.

In DaNang, the seven of us stayed in my sister's tiny house to escape the dangers in Hue. I wondered where the future would lead us. We had left all the business in Hue and moved to DaNang without any certainty ... without any guarantee we'd have a future ... without my husband. All we had was desperation.

After two weeks apart, my husband finally got a break to come visit us in DaNang. Because the fighting was still going on, he couldn't stay, but he visited when he could. This separation lasted two long months.

Then, we heard the good news: the South Army had won back Quang Tri city from the Vietcong. Dinh then led us back to Hue. Our desperate fear abated, and we enjoyed an eventful, short, and happy period. The business started again, and I had another daughter in 1973. We named her Phuong-Anh.

When she was eight months old, Phuong-Anh was on the run with me from Hue to DaNang when Hue was again attacked by the Vietcong. Before Phuong-Anh was born, we had also adopted a teenage boy whose name was Minh. Because Dinh was on active duty, Minh escorted us to DaNang this time. He was a hard-working boy. He came from a less-privileged-class family who was living in the countryside. Because we adopted him and provided him with food to eat and sent him to school, Minh, in return, treated us as his own family. He called me Aunty and my husband Sir.

With Minh's assistance, I arranged for the seven of us to move. It was a hot day in Vietnam, about thirty-five degrees Celsius. We were all in the back of a truck. To block the sun, the driver closed the back with a curtain. Thirsty and hungry, my children were worn out. In the truck, Phuc started complaining. Because I was under so much stress and my patience was reaching its limit, I spanked Phuc on his behind to teach him to be quieter. I was shocked when he screamed. I didn't think I had spanked him that hard.

I rarely spanked my children and was surprised that Phuc's reaction was so strong. Then he threw up; I was aghast to see many rubber bands spew out of his mouth. I learned he had found the rubber bands with his sister, and apparently he swallowed them without thinking. With so many children to oversee, I didn't know when Phuc swallowed the rubber bands. My oldest daughter took the rubber bands with her to have something to share with her cousins when we got to DaNang.

This time, we stayed with my sister Le for three weeks.

My husband often came to visit. Every time I expected to see him, I prayed Dinh would make it safely past the Hai Van Hill, where there was sometimes shooting.

After three weeks, Hue's security improved, and we were reunited. Dinh rented a car to take us back home to Hue. I felt much safer with my husband beside me and a peaceful view of Hai Van Hill with no dead bodies and no battle.

As the rice business improved over the months, we saved enough to build a new house close to my husband's camp. I enjoyed being a housewife, taking care of my five children while my husband was at work. My mother-in-law stayed with us, and we were a happy family.

At the end of 1973, my husband went to Saigon for three months to take a training course. During that time, I took care of the children by myself. While my mother-in-law helped us with the rice business, my mother lived by herself not far from us. I tried to visit my mother frequently, but because I was so busy with the children, I didn't have much time. If I needed her, she always helped me.

After the training in 1973, my husband received a promotion. He managed the oil and gas supply in Non Nuoc, a base supported by the United States. Dinh told me after the Americans withdrew, the South Vietnamese would have to fight the North alone, and it wouldn't be a fair fight because the North was supported by China and Russia.

In 1974, after another three months training in Saigon, Dinh became a manager of the oil and gas supply for the storage warehouse at Tieu Doan I, or Small Division I, about four kilometers from the center of DaNang. While he worked in DaNang, I stayed in Hue with our children. Occasionally, we visited him in DaNang, but most of the time, he visited us. The separation made 1974 a hard year for all of us.

CHAPTER 16

# Mom: On the Run Again

In March, 1975, we were among thousands of people from Central Vietnam again on the run from the Vietcong. The South lost city by city to the North, and Hue was once again pounded by the Vietcong. Many military units were defeated, and the Mang Ca Unit was in shambles. Our family made its way back to DaNang but found utter chaos. The Vietcong threatened DaNang as well, and we had to move further south. Hand-in-hand, we boarded a boat to Saigon.

My mother joined us on the run again. My mother-in-law had a plane ticket on the twenty-eighth of March and planned to meet us in Saigon. Tragically, the airport was destroyed and no commercial flights could leave. Our niece, Anh Tho's daughter, eventually helped my mother-in-law return to Hue after she couldn't join us in Saigon as planned.

From Saigon we, like millions of South Vietnamese people, fled our beloved homeland. We had suffered so much pain and loss — the deaths of my husband's brothers, Phuc's and my injuries in the Tet Offensive, the many times we had run for our lives from the Vietcong, the deaths and horrors of war we had witnessed so often, the bone-chilling fear for the safety of my husband and all of us, the never-ending stress and terror. I thought I was numb to any more sorrow. But leaving Vietnam was the saddest time in my life. I left behind my mother, my mother-in-law, my sister Le, and many other loved ones. Not only did we leave behind our loved ones, but also we lost all the properties we had built for over ten years. Ten years of hard work with tears and sorrows — ten years of our hearts and souls. With hearts full of pain, love, and hope, we left our pasts behind in Vietnam.

## CHAPTER 17

# Dad: We Lost the War

In 1974, I became manager of a military gas supply warehouse in DaNang after I finished a short advanced training course in Saigon. Nga stayed in Hue with my mother and took care of our five children. I tried to go home every weekend to see my family, but the visits became sporadic as the battles between the North and the South heated up.

It was early March 1975. Nga trembled in fear when she heard on the news that the communists had gained control in Quang Tri. Our neighbors, most of whom had relatives in DaNang, prepared to move further south.

In the middle of March, I sent a telegram to ask Nga to bring our children and both our mothers to DaNang as soon as possible. I received no response. Several days went by, and I still didn't have any news from my family. I was busy with many deadlines on the distribution schedule, but I was very worried about the safety of my family. I asked my subordinate Chien to arrange for a taxicab to Hue to move my family further south. Instead Chien volunteered to go, so I could take care of business.

He later told me when he went back to Hue, he saw chaos everywhere. Our house was close to the military camp, an optimal target for attacks by the communists. When he arrived, Chien told Nga and our mothers they had to pack within an hour to head south. With his help, Nga led the five children and our mothers from the house on March 19th. The taxicab moved like a turtle because the road was so crowded.

Nga panicked when she heard gunshots and mine explosions not far from the road. During the drive along the Hai Van Hill, she had a severe headache from the chaos of everyone fleeing from the communists. Images of the Tet Offensive haunted her memory. Five children clung to Nga's arms while our mothers sat silently in the car.

Chien comforted Nga by climbing on the top of the slow-moving taxi to survey the surrounding area. He told her, "I promise that I will protect you. You and your children are safe with me. If I have to die to protect you and your family, it will be my honor, and I will be happy to die to save you."

I will never forget Chien's kindness, courage, and loyal action. I remember our times together in Vietnam when he often drove me on business trips. One time, our car collided with a wire fence along the freeway because of the slippery road, but with his fast reaction and calm attitude, we were both safe. Throughout the years, he treated us like his own family, and I have to thank him for his loyalty and bravery. Without him, I'm not sure how we would have been able to move my family to DaNang.

Nga told me, "I was so terrified. There was so much chaos, and I kept remembering the Tet Offensive. I might not have made it without Chien's help."

It took more than half a day before the South Army could clear out the Hai Van Hill. Then the taxi could move forward. The long day on the road with no air conditioning in the car exhausted my family, but they finally made it to DaNang. It was almost dinner time, and I was waiting at the taxi station to greet them. Chien said goodbye to us and asked me for several days off to take care of his family. He had actually put our family's safety before his own family's welfare, and I don't know what I ever did to deserve this special treatment. We were very blessed!

DaNang could have fallen to the communists at any point. My family came to stay with me inside the gas station while I searched for a rental room nearby. We did not know how long we would need the temporary housing. We did not know that within a month we would have to say goodbye to Hue forever.

I had to wake up in the middle of the night to follow-up with the security guards. This often gave Nga nightmares about the war. Her fears increased and my job grew busier when the inventory reached over a million liters of gas.

One day, Nga happened to chat with a soldier at my camp. She asked him, "Where would be the best place for us to hide when the rockets are launched toward us?"

The soldier smiled innocently and replied, "There is no place to hide. We'll all be dead if there's an explosion."

Nga already had enough nightmare images about the fighting, bombing, tanks, guns, and battles. Now she had new nightmares of the gas station exploding and the entire family being destroyed instantly. The new image caused her to break down, and she insisted I move the family away from the gas station unit.

I rented a small house about one kilometer from the camp. I couldn't stay with my family outside the camp because policy required me to be on guard every night. During the days, I took lunch and dinner breaks to see Nga and my family, then I drove back to the camp after dinner. Each time I left the house, my mother and Nga became very nervous.

Two days after my family arrived in DaNang, we heard the communists had gained complete control in Hue, and they were ready to attack further south. People in DaNang were extremely cautious. Messages about missing persons and information about searches were broadcast and posted everywhere. One week after moving to the rental house, I realized we couldn't settle in DaNang, and I made a plan for my family to migrate to Saigon. We could only buy two airline tickets to Saigon, so my mother told us she and one of our nieces, Tho's daughter, would use the tickets and join us in Saigon. I should try to organize transportation for all my other family members.

I took my mother's advice and tried all means to make arrangements for my family. It was almost impossible to rent cars or boats because everyone was leaving DaNang to move further south. We were glad to find my sister Giao and her family in DaNang. Partnering with Giao's family, we rented a small boat to Saigon. A day before the departure date, the boat owner cancelled our trip, saying the boat was unavailable; we knew that meant he had a better offer. But we didn't know that, because of this cancellation, my sister Giao and her family would be among the ones who were left behind in Vietnam.

Nga kept asking me, "What can we do to save the family? It will be like the end of the world if the communists gain control of DaNang. I can't forget the Tet Offensive — what our family has been through! We can't live under communists!"

"I know. I know. I'm doing my best to get the family out as soon as I can."

Confused and frustrated, I drove to the other side of Thach Han River to check for the latest news. Adding to my frustrations, my boss told me I should be ready for military commands and that the soldiers should be the last to leave DaNang. He added I could not leave the unit until he released final orders from upper management.

When I reported to the unit on the twenty-seventh, I didn't see the Commander-in-Chief anywhere. I also learned from local officers there was a big ship directed to transport as much of the gas supply as possible to Saigon because there was news that DaNang would soon fall to the Vietcong. I searched for the ship's station and learned it was stationed in Thach Han River on the Bach Dang drive. Realizing there was no time to lose, I went home to drive my family and my mother-in-law to the ship. I said goodbye to my mother and wished her a good flight. I promised to find her at our relative's house when we got to Saigon, not knowing it was the last time I would ever see her.

Crowds waited along the Thach Han River. There were two ferries adjacent to the military boat where we were headed. People were running for their lives, and we were too. We had to cross the bridge where people were hustling in the midst of a press. The crush made it very difficult to elbow onto the bridge. I don't know how long it took us to get on the military ship, but we finally made it.

The ship had come to DaNang to move the gas supply to Saigon, but because of the urgency of people fleeing to South Vietnam, the ship took civilians on board. Speaking through a megaphone, the captain reminded all of the soldiers they should be the last ones to leave. If any officer got caught leaving the unit, he would suffer military discipline. After helping everyone in my family find a corner of the ship to sit down, I told Nga it was time for me to return to Non Nuoc, where my unit was stationed. I was a soldier, and I needed to follow military orders.

Back at Non Nuoc, my unit was silently dismissed. I heard over the loudspeaker the message of the quartermaster chief officer, which reminded us about our duties to protect the South. I learned that the message was only a recording which was scheduled to broadcast every fifteen minutes to keep the unit together. I realized, though I had tried my best to be a soldier, it was time for me to be with my family.

Shaking hands with Chien, my loyal subordinate, I left the camp to join my family on the ship. I told him it was time for him to place his family in first priority, and I hoped we would run into each other one day when the country became more peaceful. However, after leaving Vietnam, I have had no success in contacting Chien again. It would be nice to have a reunion with him.

Nga was totally stressed when the captain announced that the ship was ready to depart to Saigon. I was not there to be with her and our children. The situation changed almost every second, and the frequent changes added to Nga's confusion and fears. Then she heard the captain's voice again, this time a cancellation message. The military ship would not move south as planned.

Depressed and worried she wouldn't be able to find me again, Nga cried. My mother-in-law and the children were puzzled. Nga didn't know what to do. She expected me to come back to join her. Finally she decided to wait for me. The children were so tired they fell asleep. Nga and my mother-in-law patiently waited for me at the same place I had left them. They did not get off the ship, despite the captain's cancellation announcement. It was one of the best decisions Nga ever made.

On the way back to the ship, I learned from one officer that the captain had to announce the cancellation because the military ship could not afford to carry over its permitted weight and could not depart with people continuing to hustle on board. When I got back, most of the people were leaving the ship area, and the crowd was still in disorder. I remembered how hard it had been to escort all of my family on board. Nga almost fell in the water when we first attempted to elbow through lines of people on the bridge. I told myself if I was lucky enough to find Nga and kids still on board, I would never leave them again.

Next, I saw many people headed back to the military ship. I later learned there was a silent arrangement for selective members to be on board in the middle of this chaos. The captain had just announced the cancellation so the ship would have a lighter weight for safety. When enough people decided to get off the ship to find different means of transportation, he would be ready to depart. I didn't know if Nga and my family had left the ship or not. I was very worried when I saw several police officers start closing the gates that blocked the entrance. If my family was not still on board, we would not be able to leave DaNang. It was very late, almost midnight of March 29th.

When I boarded the ship, I found my family in the same area where I'd left them. It was a great reunion — I was so happy to see them, and Nga acted as if we hadn't seen each other for centuries! While the kids were sleeping, Nga couldn't help but complain about my long absence. I felt guilty for leaving my family and promised my wife I wouldn't leave her alone again. At the time, I didn't know my mother was stuck at the DaNang airport. If I'd known, I would have gone back to take her with us.

About fifteen minutes after I was on board, we heard bombings and gunshots near us. The captain commanded the ship to depart with about a hundred families on board. We were heading to Saigon, leaving behind the rockets' lights and gunshots and DaNang's chaos. Later we learned if we had been ten minutes later, the ship might have been destroyed like many other ships and boats in the area. Many people died on the day we left.

It was about one o'clock in the morning, on the 30th of March, 1975, when we left DaNang for Saigon. People on the ship were too tired to talk. Everyone slept after a long day fighting for their spots on board. Nga gained some strength and lost some stress with me to help her take care of the children. As my mother-in-law sat with us, I thought of my mother and wondered if she had arranged a place for us with our relatives in Saigon. I didn't know I had just missed my last chance to take care of her.

In the middle of the night, we suddenly heard shouting, "*Ban bo di, ban bo di,*" or "Shoot him down, shoot him down," and "*Nem xuong bien di, nem xuong bien di,*" or "Throw him in the water, throw him in the sea." The security guards rushed down to the ship's basement, and they caught several men fighting over a smoking cigarette. These people did not know the ship was a military gas supply ship, and they didn't realize how dangerous it could be if the lighter sparked the ship — we would die instantly. After lots of shouting and warnings, the security guards kept the cigarette smokers under control. The guards warned the smokers they could be deported in any port or even be thrown in the water if they weren't careful. The incident exhausted everyone, especially Nga, but she was too frightened to sleep.

My family didn't have a good spot on board. We sat on the balcony which had no cover. A small amount of dry food was distributed to each family. Nga and I didn't dare eat so our children would have more food. The odor of gas blended with the smell of food made the situation worse. We struggled for a day, passing several small islands, until the ship reached Quy Nhon, a small town about 650 kilometers from Saigon.

On the ship, we were lucky to meet one of my subordinates, Sergeant Luong. When the ship docked briefly at Quy Nhon port to cool off the engine, Luong volunteered to go ashore to find food and drink. He told us Quy Nhon people were very hospitable; they greeted the Central immigrants at the ports and handed out food and drinks for free. Luong used a raft on a single straw boat to reach the inside land to obtain enough food and drink for all of us. This food helped us to last until the ship came to Vung Tau, a popular camp area near Saigon.

The kindness of people like Chien, Luong, and many Quy Nhon civilians amazed us, especially in the midst of chaos, war, and fleeing from the communists. Among the bad and the evil, I appreciated the simple goodness shown by many people in South Vietnam during this ugly time. We were very blessed to have so much help from so many friends at all the right times!

The sea distance from DaNang to Saigon is about 1100 kilometers. It took us two nights and a day to reach Vung Tau port. During the second night, our ship had a minor accident with another ship which was also on the move to Saigon. Luckily, both ships were safe and no damage was obvious. Nga kept thinking about the minor collision, since she was so conscious about how much gas the ship was carrying. Her conversation with the soldier about a possible explosion made her extremely nervous during the trip. The tension was increased because neither Nga nor I knew where we were going. We had no clue of what the future would hold for our family, but we hoped we all could make it to Saigon to reunite with my mother.

We finally saw our destination. Vung Tau was an R&R (Rest and Recreation) area for American soldiers during the war. The beaches were beautiful, and the local people were helpful. Nga felt relieved knowing that there were staff greeting us along the beaches, handing out food, medicine, and drinks. There were monks, Catholic priests and nuns, and social workers to take care of the refugees, most of whom came from Hue and DaNang. A bus transferred us from the beach directly to Trai Gia Binh, or Camp for Military Officers' Families twenty kilometers away from Saigon.

We stayed at Trai Gia Binh for over two weeks. During this time, all I could do was hope. I hoped the South might receive international help to regain control in DaNang and Hue, so I could return home. The camp was very organized, which encouraged me. During this month, we were assigned to share a room with two other families. There were fourteen people staying in the room, which was furnished with several compact day beds. There were other officers, so I could exchange some information with them. I hoped to find a way to connect with my unit in Saigon.

At first, everyone was happy to be safe and rescued. After much uncertainty, we felt secure at Trai Gia Binh camp, which appeared to be highly protected from the communists. I could see the happiness on Nga's face — she didn't mind taking care of our five children with limited space at the camp. Then a week went by, and Nga got sick. She was overworked and stressed with worry and uncertainty about our future.

I tried to contact my unit in Saigon for help and contacted my relatives for news of my mother. I had my cousin HD's address where I planned to unite with her. When I reached HD's house, I learned my mother could not leave DaNang as planned because the airport was destroyed and no commercial airplanes could fly out. From a relative, I learned my mother and my niece tagged along with several neighbors back to Hue. Hue then fell into Vietcong hands, and I helplessly wished for my mother's safety.

In the turmoil of being separated from my mother, I was lucky to reunite with my sister Tran. Tran's husband, who I called Older Brother H, was a high ranking officer, and he recommended we leave Vietnam. He predicted Vietnam would be taken over by the communists since the South army was too confused to do any solid planning. Both our families went to stay at HD, our cousin's home.

My cousin HD was a businesswoman in Saigon. She had a four-story house on Phan Dinh Phung Street with several helpers and a housekeeper. A couple of weeks before the fall of Saigon, HD went on a business trip to Paris, and she has remained in France ever since. Before she left Vietnam, she asked her housekeeper to let us and other relatives stay in her house if we ever needed a place in Saigon. Tran's family had arrived at HD's house several hours before us and stayed on the third floor. We were the last group of HD's relatives to arrive in Saigon. The lower levels of the house were full of relatives, some of whom we had never met before. The housekeeper guided us to the fourth floor and said he had saved the space for us, keeping my cousin HD's promise.

We stayed at the Phan Dinh Phung house until the day we left Vietnam. It was very hard for Nga to move up and down four flights of stairs every day. We didn't have much money, but we did have enough for food. When I reported to headquarters in Saigon, I was awarded a month's salary to get my family going again. My infantry unit recalled all officers to headquarters in Saigon and started our meetings for future operations. With my humble stipend, Nga and I went to Ben Thanh market to buy dinner for all of us. Since the day we left DaNang, it was the first decent meal we had eaten. I remember how excited my children were when they saw two big roasted ducks for dinner. It was a special meal, and the family was happy — for a short time.

However, we couldn't enjoy our happiness very long. The day after I received my allowance, I started to see people leaving Saigon; many officers in my unit were not reporting to work. Rumors spread that Saigon would soon fall to the Vietcong. I saw worry and concern in Nga's eyes. The reunion with Nga's cousin TNP and his wife in Saigon made her worry more. TNP's wife told us everyone was trying to escape from Saigon and nothing could be guaranteed. Everyone seemed to act differently. Many relatives and friends hinted they would like to leave Vietnam, but none of them told us how and when. From the balcony, we saw people moving in a hurry; many carried heavy luggage and bags. We could feel the tension everywhere.

Nga begged, "Let's find a way to leave Vietnam as soon as possible."

At first, I didn't want to listen to her. I thought of my elderly mother who was still stranded in Hue. I thought of the possible future reconstruction of Vietnam if the South could get more international help. I told Nga, "I couldn't forgive myself for leaving my mother behind. Besides I don't have any connections to leave the country."

We talked about leaving Saigon for a couple of days until I observed Nga's emotions, especially when she watched people running back and forth on the streets. From the balcony of the fourth floor, we watched several relatives move out of the house where we stayed.

Nga said, "Everyone is leaving. Even our relatives are leaving and don't even take time to say goodbye to us. It's time for us to join the flow, before the communists arrive, before it's too late. Think about our children. Think about their futures. We can't let them live under the communists. We have to put their futures before anything else."

When I saw everyone on the lower two floors had left without saying goodbye to us, I was convinced it was time for us to leave. Even though I thought of my mother, I had no means to contact her.

The South had already lost both Hue and DaNang, and Saigon was about to go, too. It was time for us to leave; at least Nga and my children would have a chance for better futures. Finally I agreed with Nga, and we started packing. We packed everything we had in two small bags. My sister Tran and her family joined us. We all stood outside the house, looking for a means of transportation.

It was April 29th, 1975. We didn't know where we could find a car or taxi. Every single taxi appeared to be taken, and all the cars on the streets were fully packed. The gunshots and traffic sounds made us nervous. People were on the run with no clear direction. I carried Phuong-Anh in my right arm and held Dzung with my left hand. I told Phuc to hold on to my belt and cautioned him not to turn loose for any reason. I also urged him to pay close attention to the family so we didn't lose each other. My mother-in-law joined us, and she helped Nga take care of the two girls. Nga held Ngoc and Thuy on each side, hand-in-hand.

There were fifteen of us in my family and Tran's family looking for transportation to the airport or the seaport. Perhaps a miracle led us in this chaotic time. A young couple, the gentleman in a white shirt and blue trousers and the lady in a white dress, stopped their Jeep in front of us. I never had a chance to ask their names. The gentleman asked if we knew the way to Khanh Hoi port. He said there was an overseas commercial ship docked there, and he and his wife needed directions to get there. He added, if we wished, he could give us a ride to Khanh Hoi as well.

Tran's husband H, who was in the military and often went to Saigon for business, knew the city well. He immediately volunteered to guide the couple to the port. H told us he had feared we'd lost our last chance to leave Vietnam, and we were lucky to find a way out by helping these people.

We could not fit all the people in the Jeep and had to divide the group. We debated who should be in the first group to go to Khanh Hoi with the young couple whose names we didn't even know. Finally Nga and I agreed to let Tran's family go first and then H should come back to pick us up. It was the only way all of us could get out of Saigon. One of Tran's daughters H-P, who was very close to me, offered to wait for the second trip.

It took more than an hour for H to come back with the Jeep. We feared he wouldn't be able to come back for us in the chaos. Perhaps H pushed himself since his daughter H-P had stayed with us, as I was then her favorite uncle. Our family and my niece jumped for joy and climbed on the Jeep before H turned and began the journey back to the Khanh Hoi port.

Traveling back and forth took time and extreme patience because the roads were too crowded for cars to move. In addition, the number of spaces on board was limited, and people had no time to go back and forth to pick up passengers like H did. It was a miracle he didn't abandon us. We were, again, very lucky to have good family members.

## CHAPTER 18

# Dad: Becoming Refugees

... After my mother-in-law left, the population on the Anh Tuan ship kept increasing. There were several hundred people on board when the captain and the ship's staff decided to leave. We departed from Vietnam at five o'clock in the afternoon of April 29th, 1975, less than a day before Saigon fell to the communists. With me were Nga and our five children — Ngoc was eight, Phuc was seven, Thuy was five, Dzung was three, and Phuong-Anh was two. We left everything behind. There was no certainty, but there was hope.

After we had crawled through the circle barbed wire and successfully crossed the narrow plank bridge onto the Anh Tuan ship, we sat on the corner of the boat, not knowing what the future would hold. I worried about the safety of my elderly mother. I watched my children who were so tired. On the sea, I could hear the restless ocean around us. My first night away from Saigon was memorable. I no longer saw the chaos, but my head spun with memories: the noise of rockets, mine explosions, and gunshots; sounds of people running for their lives; and the cries of hungry children. After all these years, I was grateful to be alive, but I felt a deep sorrow for my country.

I had a chance to talk with several families on the ship. Some latecomers told us the communists were attacking Saigon; the city was very chaotic; and people outside the port were on the run for their lives. Some people said they had hoped to be evacuated by air via Tan Son Nhut Airport, but the Vietcong had destroyed the runways. The lines in front of the Embassy Building were too long and crowded for hope of escape. Some told us exceptions were supposed to be made for high-ranking officers and military personnel who had worked closely with the Americans, but these could not be granted because of the lack of transportation. The Anh Tuan was only one of many ships — all fully packed with Southerners and Central region refugees like us — that departed Saigon during the last days.

After a good night's sleep on board, I woke up the next morning beside my children and Nga. While having break-fast provided by the ship's staff, we heard on the radio that President Duong Van Minh had asked the South Army to surrender. Saigon was then fully controlled by the commu-nists. Someone next to us cried, "*Minh mat nuoc roi.*" or "We lost our country."

Someone else shouted, "*Minh thua roi. Minh that su mat nuoc roi.*" "We lost the war. We already lost our country."

There was no more Saigon ... and no more Hue — the old Saigon and the beloved Hue where I grew up were no more. When the President of South Vietnam Duong Van Minh announced that the South Vietnamese had surrendered to the Vietcong, his Southern accent battered my ears and hurt my heart. I silently said goodbye forever to Saigon, to Hue, and to my mother. I said goodbye forever to my motherland. The possibility of coming back seemed too remote to imagine. Everyone on the ship mourned for Saigon. We mourned for Vietnam.

Vietnam had been very beautiful. However, I witnessed

many sad historical events, and we went through many traumatic experiences. As mentioned earlier, I was a teenager in high school when Vietnam was divided into the North and the South. During my youth, I experienced the loss of many loved ones. Whether a happy place or not, Vietnam is a place in my heart, where I left my mother behind.

I didn't know how the Vietcong would treat her. They had killed my father-in-law, caused Nga and Phuc to be injured, and destroyed many other families during the Tet Offensive. I was sad for my nation, where education was controlled by food, and where fighting continued over the years. It was sad when thousands of years of tradition were ruined by the tough ideals of communism. Experience made me skeptical about communism, but all I could do during this difficult time was hope. I couldn't overcome the hardships without hope. After many sad historical events, I still hoped Vietnam could find peace.

Other sad events such as the Red Fire Summer in 1972 separated us for months when weekends had been the only times I could see my family. I risked my life driving past the Hai Van Hill for weekly family visits. I don't know how Nga handled it when our four children suffered severe flu on the run. I witnessed how people's characters were shaped and how miserably they suffered. Among the strong people that I admire, I admire Nga the most.

1973 was another sad time for us when the Vietcong again attacked the South. The communists once again attacked several cities and towns along the seventeenth parallel, including Hue. We were again on the run facing many obstacles which Nga described. We spent a tough week in DaNang, when Nga again took care of five children, including Phuong-Anh who had just been born.

From 1968 to 1975, the winds of chaos roared through my country and through my family. Vietnam and the Truong-Nhu family faced war and communism, death and separation, danger and destruction. Because of these sad historical events, Nga learned to lead our family in her sweet way. She was a silent leader who I depended on during these years. I would not be the same without Nga's support. Despite all the hardships I faced, I recognized a wonderful part of life: I realized how much I cherish Nga and my family; they are my hopes and dreams coming true.

Now we were all on a boat headed away from Vietnam.

# CHAPTER 19

# Mom: A Housewife Adapts to Refugee Life

I was very sad when we escaped Saigon at the end of April in 1975. We rushed to a commercial ship named Anh Tuan in the Saigon harbor. Nearly full of people when we boarded, the Anh Tuan allowed our family and hundreds of others to escape the Vietcong. When we said farewell to my mother and left the harbor, Saigon was in its highest state of chaos. Thousands of military troops from the North were invading the capital of the South. We just left Vietnam, not knowing what the future held or where it would lead us.

Above our heads was a cloudy sky, and beneath us was the endless sea. The Anh Tuan ship was small, and we didn't have much room. This was nature's ultimate test of human suffering and patience. I saw water everywhere with no land in sight. The horizon was far away, like an illusion in a novel I read a long time ago.

We were on the sea for more than two days, and I saw the sun set and rise. I used to love watching the sun set;

however, when fatigue and hunger struck, Mother Nature was no longer attractive. Days on the sea with limited food and fresh water exhausted everyone. Our children were affected by dehydration. Phuong-Anh either slept or cried; perhaps she cried more than she slept because of starvation. The sun took its toll on us all. Drinking water was scarce. I tried to close my eyes to have some rest and hoped to let my mind find some peaceful moments. At least I had my family with me. No matter what happened, we had each other.

The noise of people around us woke me. Then I heard the captain announce we had reached the American Subic Bay Naval Base. Finally, Buddha answered my prayers. We were safe in the Philippines, away from the communists, where we would be assisted by the Americans and UN officials.

The American ship that rescued us was the biggest ship I had ever seen. The soldiers used a ladder to pull us up one by one. We were provided with food, fresh water, and showers. My husband and my son Phuc enjoyed the shower with fresh water on the American ship. It broke my heart just to observe their happiness over a simple shower. It was like an escape from hell to heaven when we were rescued and welcomed by Americans in the Philippines.

The ship arrived in Subic Bay at noon. American soldiers guided us on land. The elders and babies were carried piggyback or held gently. A young soldier held my hand to help me walk on the shore. American soldiers also carried heavy bags for Vietnamese refugees. I was moved to tears by the help from Americans I'd never met before.

The refugee camp in Subic Bay was very organized. The walk from the ship to the refugee camp was pretty far for my injured leg, but I felt relief because of the hospitality of social workers and American soldiers. People moved slowly to the camp because of the long journey to peace. We finally arrived at the refugee camp and took care of the required paperwork.

Social workers at the camp told us we had two choices: one was to depart immediately to Guam, and the other was to stay at this Subic Bay camp for a couple days to rest before going to Guam. Both Dinh and I wanted to depart immediately. After multiple uncertainties and constant moves, the sooner our family could settle in a safe place and start over, the better for all of us.

Because we chose to depart for Guam immediately, we didn't spend much time at Subic Bay. But we will never forget our first impression of America — the humanity and compassion poured out on us. For the half a day we stayed in Subic Bay, I felt joy to be safe with my family. I was happy just to have escaped from war-torn Vietnam to a safer place, but sadness for our mothers still tore at my heart.

Many people chose to be transferred to Guam immediately, so we stood in line to board the C130 plane. Since it was a freight plane rather than a passenger plane, there were no seats. We were seated by traveling groups on the floor and provided with small bags of snacks and drinks. During the flight, which lasted more than four hours, the American soldiers walked back and forth to oversee everything and to ask if we were comfortable or needed anything. The hours passed by really fast since I had many new things to experience. The hospitality of Americans once again warmed my wounded heart.

Arriving in Guam, we were greeted by the volunteer staff and transported by buses to the refugee camp. While on the bus, I observed Guam and its people. At a small kiosk, I saw people in line buying food. Most people were traveling the clean streets by cars. Guam's appearance was peaceful, and the weather was perfect. I reminisced about days on the sea and felt so sorry for us, for the Vietnamese people. A peaceful life in Vietnam was now impossible.

When the bus stopped at the gate, I saw tents lining the

road from the main entrance as far as I could see. Hundreds of refugees who had arrived earlier greeted us. Dinh and I were anxious to see the camp and wondered how long we would stay there. I felt lucky to have escaped from the communists, but I wondered if my mother and mother-in-law were safe. I missed both of them deeply even though I did not mention anything about them. My family was my first priority.

We were all in lines to fill out paperwork. Along the lines were tables filled with soft drinks and snacks. Dzung, who was three years old at the time, was the most excited kid. He took a Coca-Cola® can, but he accidentally dropped it. The can hit my foot, scratched my skin, and caused minor bleeding.

Pointing to my foot, I asked one of the Red Cross members for help. My gesture was just to ask for a bandage, but I didn't know any English at the time. The staff saw that I had a bleeding foot and immediately called the ambulance to take me to the hospital. I tried to explain to them it wasn't serious, but they didn't understand me. The ambulance arrived, and several emergency workers rolled out a wheel chair. We were all confused but didn't understand their intentions. Then they loaded me in the ambulance and drove me away, straight to the camp's clinic. The doctors and nurses performed a series of tests on me. Because of the language barrier, I was totally confused. Worse, I couldn't contact my husband because no one around me spoke or understood Vietnamese. I stayed at the clinic overnight. The nurse brought me dinner, but I couldn't eat much.

I was amazed how friendly the American nurses were. Every couple of hours, the nurse came and checked on me. The medical staff was both professional and friendly. At the time, I didn't understand American workers worked different shifts. All the nurses looked the same to me, so I thought the same nurses took care of me day and night without breaks. Later when I learned more about American customs, I still appreciated what the nurses had done for me. I was so impressed with the services they provided me. They were so professional it was hard for me to make the distinctions between different people.

After reviewing all the test results and making sure I was okay, a nurse told me I could go back to my family's tent. I wanted to go back to my tent but didn't know where it was. People at the clinic finally arranged for a Jeep to take me back to the main office. A young Red Cross agent drove me to the office, and he asked me to write down my name and my husband's name on a piece of paper. I believed they'd call Dinh over the intercom to pick me up, so I waited.

After four hours of waiting at the Red Cross office, I'd heard nothing. There was no news from my husband. It was noon, and I felt hungry and became more and more worried as time passed. Every hour in the afternoon, the Red Cross office announced my name via the intercom, but Dinh didn't hear the announcement. Not only was I worried, but I was also bored and stiff from just sitting in the office. So I started walking around to stretch my legs and body.

I saw a very young soldier. He walked toward the office, near where I stood. He looked at me and recognized my confusion. He stopped and asked me something in English, perhaps asking me if he could help me with anything. I saw he held a soda in his hand. Because I was thirsty and hungry, I pointed to the can and then pointed to my mouth. The young soldier smiled and gave me his soda. I took it without thinking. I felt much better after I drank almost half the can.

Then, I realized it was rude to ask the young soldier for his drink, so I returned the half-empty can to him! He smiled and took it back, probably wondering what I meant. Perhaps he was confused by my strange action; he drank a little bit from the can and gave me back the rest. Not being able to communicate with me, the soldier walked away, leaving me with the half-full can of soda. He probably said goodbye, and I waved back. I then continued to wait for Dinh.

Finally my husband showed up with our five children. Phuong-Anh jumped up and ran to hug me as if we hadn't seen each other for months! We all walked back to our tent and wondered if we'd missed dinner since we were so late. Fortunately, the cook learned we didn't get to eat due to my emergency stay at the hospital; therefore, he didn't mind preparing leftovers for us. What an eventful day for me!

Dinh told me when the ambulance took me to the hospital, he'd had to manage five children and complete the application forms for all of us. Our family was assigned a tent far away from the clinic. Because it was difficult to understand the announcement over the intercom, he didn't hear it until 7:00 PM. Even knowing some English, his listening skills were not good at the time.

We lived in Guam for about two months. Each time the buses stopped at the main gates, we, like other Vietnamese refugees, ran to the fence to see if one of our relatives or friends had arrived. Dinh and I missed Vietnam a great deal, so we found the refugee experience difficult. Several families had brought small radios, and we gathered around them to listen for news of our homeland. We learned Saigon had fallen to the Vietcong and many people had died when they were on the sea searching for freedom.

Some nights I woke up and discovered my face covered with tears though I didn't know how long I'd been crying. I had so much time to remember the past and think of my mother, and the sorrow pierced my heart all the time we were in Guam. I tried not to express my sadness outside, so my husband and my children could have more peace. Time has helped to ease my pain.

From Guam, our family was transferred to Pennsylvania, to the Fort Indiantown Gap Refugee Camp. Dinh and the kids adapted to the new culture much faster than I did. They loved to eat American food! Every day at camp, we were in line for food and took lots of eggs, oranges, and leftovers back to the tent. It was hard for me to eat because I was not used to the American food, and I missed the taste of a normal Vietnamese meal, with fish sauce as an essential ingredient. At the camp, we ate fish occasionally; however, the American way of preparing fish is much different than the Vietnamese way. I couldn't eat much fish at the camp even though I missed the fish sauce! The cooks were surprised because people tended not to eat much on the days fish was served as the main course; I was not alone in having different tastes from Western cooking.

## CHAPTER 20

# Dad: From the Lost Roads

After every communist attack, we went on a lost road. Most times we had to start from the beginning and ended with nothing until we reached "Rome."

We lost everything, but more importantly, we managed to keep our family together. Many families who made it to the States were not perfect like us: Some lost their fathers; some lost their mothers; some lost their siblings; and some died at sea. Under the communist regime, many families suffered for many years.

On the run, I learned more about the value of friendship and family. I learned to empathize with less fortunate people, and I became more humble. I cherished life because it taught me powerful lessons. I hoped for my children to have better futures. Hopes could be like the ancient systems linking "Rome" with its most distant provinces. I thought of America as "Rome," where we started our lives again. The Roman roads we went through often were not straight lines as we wished, but were efficiently constructed by love and trust.

We were not the only ones on the lost roads.

The voice coming through the megaphone from the ship of

the 7ᵗʰ Naval Fleet stated if we were immigrants, we would be safe. The voice said sailors would take us on board one by one, as long as we followed orders.

Nga's injured leg and our small children made it challenging for us to be transported from the small ship to the larger ship. The Navy used a hanging ladder approximately twenty feet long to pull everyone up. I had to climb the ladder to get on board, and then help my children and Nga do the same.

Images of falling back into the ocean and receiving no help made Nga panic. She was very intimidated by the long hanging ladder, but she struggled to be pulled up the side of the ship. Relief washed over her like the waves when she was safely lifted on board by the sailors.

I have never forgotten our first American meal. Each person received a Ration, C type, like the dry foods American soldiers often carried with them. I saw American soldiers hold and play with my children despite the difference in languages. I knew that we would have more opportunities in America. I was amazed we were not alone, even when we thought life was almost over for us.

We met the Ngo family in May of 1975, at Guam's refugee camp. We developed empathy for each others' needs and didn't feel so lonely in this world. The couple had no children at the time. Lang Ngo was twenty-six, and his wife Diep was twenty-four. I learned on the first day we met that Lang and Diep had made an escape to "Nowhere" and also couldn't believe they could be rescued by the Americans. Like us, the Ngos didn't know what the future would hold for them.

Lang was a naval officer and at the last minute decided to leave Vietnam from Phu Quoc Island. Phu Quoc, located in the South and linked to the Pacific Ocean, was the home of Lang's unit. Lang and Diep were among tens of thousands of people who were rescued by the American Challenger Boat, a large commercial boat that could hold over 500 tons. Without children, the Ngos' journey to search for freedom was less challenging than ours, but Lang told me all they brought with them was 36,000 dong, the South Vietnamese currency that no longer had monetary value.

One thing I admired about Lang was his upbeat personality, even when our self-esteem was tortured by life's daily hardships. He liked to joke — he told me it kept our life less serious so we could be happier.

Our families' friendship grew when Lang considered me as his older brother. What a fortune in life to have a family friend to share homesickness and fill each other's days in the lonely world. Every day at camp, Lang and Diep joined our family in line for food. I remember Lang always told jokes that made everyone smile, and he used paper napkins to create cute little hats for our children. Lang's humor made us forget the summer heat, and his caring manner made us feel more comfortable and less homesick. I felt very lucky our family had such great companions and friends who helped make our roads to Rome much shorter.

The nostalgic feelings about our time in Vietnam enhanced our friendship. Lang was a social smoker, and more than once, I shared some of my humble resources of cigarettes with Lang at the camp, of course, without Diep's knowledge. When we left the camp for Maryland, we often sent them letters and kept in contact. They have lived in several states since then because of their jobs, and recently Lang worked in Wisconsin. They have two children who have their own families now. Last time I talked with Lang, he told me he had become a grandfather when his daughter in Tennessee had a baby.

When we were in the camp in Fort Indiantown Gap in Pennsylvania, Vietnamese immigrants often gathered at churches and pagodas, depending on their religion. We often went to the pagodas. We believed we were blessed by Buddha, especially when we met Nga's cousin TNP and his wife during a pagoda visit. It was a happy surprise!

TNP's mother is my mother-in-law's cousin. We had not been in contact since the fall of Saigon. One day, while Nga took care of the children at home, I went to the pagoda to pay respect to our ancestors. I saw someone who looked like TNP's wife. After a moment of doubtfulness, I came closer and recognized her. I shouted, "Mo P" or "Miss P!"

TNP's wife, no less surprised than I was, shouted back, "Anh Dinh?" or "Brother Dinh?" Mo P asked if Nga and the kids were with me and if our family had been unified. I told her everyone was safe and Nga was taking care of our children at home. Mo P added it was a blessing for Nga to make it, knowing she had an injured leg. Mo P thanked Buddha for bringing her the good news about our family.

After the ceremony at the pagoda, Mo P followed me back to the barracks at the camp to see Nga and the children. I could see Nga and Mo P's eyes moisten with tears. Mo P told us their family had been sponsored by an American family and they were currently living in Silver Spring, Maryland.

The connection between our families and many relatives who escaped from the communists became stronger. By keeping each other informed about our lives, we lessened our stress and concentrated on a positive outcome. Cousin TNP and his family moved to Houston in 1981. We call TNP Cau P and P's wife Mo P to show our family closeness. We maintain close contact, not only with Cau and Mo P, but with his daughter's family.

In addition to seeing Nga's cousin TNP and his family, we have maintained a long-term relationship with my cousin Luong. Luong's mother was a younger sister of my mother. Luong's sister lived in America before the fall of Saigon. She had married an American officer and lived in Springfield, Virginia. I can still remember when Luong's sister came to visit him at the camp — she often brought us Vietnamese dishes that she had spent hours cooking. Luong's family cheered Nga up with their positive stories about America which made her feel less lonely. It was Luong's sister who recommended our family to the church that sponsored us. We thank Luong and his sister for all their help.

We were blessed to have such great relatives and nice friends. We look back and feel extremely privileged and honored to know so many kindhearted people. We are thankful for the opportunities to learn from the church, our friends, and relatives. Without them with us on the lost roads to Rome, our journey would have been more difficult.

# CHAPTER 21

# Mom: A New Beginning

In June 1975, we went to the camp's clinic to receive immunization shots. I often vomited and felt weak but didn't know why. When I had a follow-up exam, I learned I was ten weeks pregnant. The doctor explained to me and my husband that another baby would be extremely challenging for us. He reminded us we already had five children and my health was at a very high risk if we decided to keep the baby, especially with my injured leg. He told us abortion was a common practice in America, and because of my health, we should consider that option. He added the cost of giving birth and caring for a baby outside the camp was very high, and the sooner our decision was made, the better we could plan for our future.

Dinh and I thanked the doctor for his concerns, but we refused to have the abortion. We would rather have less with our new baby than have more with the abortion. We never could imagine our lives without one of our children. We knew after they grew up, our children would appreciate the sacrifices we made. For years living with my injured leg, I'd had enough strength to take care of my children. I believed I would have enough strength to care for this child. My husband and I believed in our ability to overcome the hardships.

Through the guidance of the UN, we exchanged contacts with several relatives who lived on the East Coast. One of my cousins who lived in Washington, DC, recommended us to the Long Green Valley Church of the Brethren. For us to leave the camp and start our independent lives, we needed the church's sponsorship. It took us more than a month to finalize all the required paperwork.

At the Fort Indiantown Gap Refugee Camp, even though I couldn't speak any English, I had many Vietnamese friends. Later, Vietnamese translators and workers joined the UN staff, so I started feeling more comfortable with life at the camp. As soon as I'd made some friends, it was time for a change. I was very nervous, wondering if I would be able to function outside the camp, where I would have to communicate in English daily. We were informed of the date and time for our relocation — August 1975. We decided to start our lives outside the refugee camp under the church's sponsorship and had about a week to prepare. We were anxious about the final date and couldn't wait to settle down.

As we said goodbye to our Vietnamese friends and the staff at the camp, we were eager to meet our sponsors. We brought along with us two small suitcases. Pastor Kenneth Long and his administrative assistant, JoAnn Alderfer, came to meet us. After brief greetings and introductions, Pastor Long and JoAnn told us that it was time for us to go "home." "Going home," this sounded really strange to me. Would it be like our own home in Vietnam?

Pastor Long drove the church's station wagon. My husband sat in the front with him. JoAnn joined me and my children in the back seat. My children were very happy to receive chocolates and candies from JoAnn while I looked through the car window and observed the scenery. I was so impressed with the roads and freeways.

During the trip, Pastor Long and JoAnn asked us about our lives in Vietnam and the camps. My husband told them about the adventures we had experienced and about our mothers still in Vietnam. During this trip, I tried to avoid making any noise; I couldn't make any conversation because my husband was my interpreter. I felt uncomfortable, and my feet got tired from sitting so long.

From the Fort Indiantown Gap Refugee Camp, it took us about five hours to get to the center of Maryland, and from the center of Maryland, it took us about three hours to get to the church. Pastor Long made several stops when we came closer to the church and finally took us to the house on Harford Road.

When Pastor Long parked the car, I saw many people already at the house — most of them were from the church. JoAnn told Dinh we would stay in the Harford house temporarily until we could afford to pay our own rent; she said everyone at the church was happy to welcome us to America. She introduced me to several people; I could say "hello" and "thank you" — that was all I knew at the time.

Before the dinner started, JoAnn took me around the house to show me where everything was. Looking at the neatly-made bed with the pink comforter, I wondered if my children could keep the house neat and clean so we would not upset the sponsors' hospitality.

JoAnn said we should feel comfortable here as if it were our own home. She added we deserved to have a good start and Harford house was where we started. I was very grateful for this beginning.

All afternoon, people from the church brought us different dishes. There were so many foods, it seemed like we were having a church potluck party at the house. I was overwhelmed with the friendliness and caring manners of the church people. Part of me was still very shy, and I felt strange when most of the people gave me hugs even though they were meeting me for the first time. I was too shy to hug people back. My husband told me it was just the culture difference, and I should loosen up a little bit so I could feel less nervous.

My cousins came from Washington, DC. With their help and with my husband's limited English, I could communicate with people from the church to thank them for the food and gifts. I realized not knowing the language and culture would be a big barrier for me to overcome.

I couldn't eat much although there were so many different foods on the table. I felt lonely even though I was surrounded by so many kindhearted people.

The sponsor family stayed on the upper story while our family stayed on the first floor of the house. When everyone left, I was overwhelmed with the changes. I saw my children's excitement as they walked around the house. They were too excited to be in bed on time. After several months without a comfortable bed, I felt blessed to have a nice place to call home, even temporarily. We all shared a large master bedroom with a king size bed. Four children — Ngoc, Phuc, Thuy, and Dzung — slept on the bed, while Dinh, I, and baby Phuong-Anh slept on the floor with thick blankets. I had a very cozy feeling. I was happy for our family, but the good changes recalled memories of our early lives long ago in Vietnam.

I couldn't sleep, and looking at Dinh next to me, I saw he wasn't sleeping either. It took us a while to fall to sleep, though both of us were tired after a long day — a long day with lots of good beginnings, a long day with lots of memories.

I missed Vietnam, our mothers, friends, and other relatives. I knew I had to overcome the difficulties. This time it wouldn't be the hardship of running from the Vietcong, but it would be the hardship of overcoming the culture and language barriers. Imagining how the future would be for us, I don't know when I finally fell asleep, but it was the nicest sleep I'd had for a long time!

## CHAPTER 22

# Mom: American Life

We were lucky to get a good start from the church. Pastor Long told us he was proud of the church's history. He said it was common to see long-time-married couples in the neighborhood. Most families went to church and lived healthy lifestyles; it was rare to see divorces or drug, alcohol, or gambling habits from these families. The church sponsored at least five or six other families before and after us. It was an honor for my family to be sponsored by the church.

I had not had any good sleep since the day I left Vietnam. On the first night at our "own" home, I slept until 8:00 AM the next day. I was happy for my family. During the first weeks, people from the church helped me with daily chores. They brought me food and drinks and even cleaned the house for me. They told me I needed to rest because I was weak and pregnant. I tried to let them know I could take care of the household and I felt bad letting them serve me, but they insisted on helping.

I appreciated our friends at the church. I loved Ms. Edna Mueller. She treated me like I was her family. Ms. Mueller was such a character. I can still remember her laugh — it was like a cheerful firecracker. During our first days in Maryland, I felt less homesick and my days went much faster because of her. Naturally, she comforted my pain in her own cute way. When the church sponsored our family, they divided the sponsorship into different tasks. Different families took specific responsibilities to help us: Charles and Edna Mueller helped me and Thuy. Mr. and Mrs. Verlin Tombaugh helped Ngoc. Mr. and Mrs. Norman Bollinger helped Phuc. JoAnn and her husband Jim Alderfer helped Dzung and Phuong-Anh.

A couple of months later, the church also gave us a car — a Datsun 210 that cost about 500 dollars. That was a lot of money for us. People from the church helped Dinh obtain his driver's license. They also showed him how to maintain the car. Occasionally, when the car's engine didn't start, Mr. Norman Bollinger showed Dinh some tricks. While adapting to America, both my husband and I learned new things every day.

Days in Fallston, Maryland, were very memorable. Several days passed before I could operate the range and cook by myself. Marian from the church drove me to a Vietnamese grocery store in Virginia. I was happily surprised to see all sorts of Vietnamese ingredients in this store. Marian told me not to worry about the cost, but I just bought what we needed for a simple Vietnamese meal.

Dinh and I enjoyed our first traditional Vietnamese meal in America. The soy sauce and boiled vegetables made the meal so tasty for both of us! My children were not so impressed with the first meal I prepared in Maryland, and I understood where they were coming from. There were big differences between Western and Eastern foods, and they were already developing Western tastes.

Later after my husband learned how to drive, he often took me to Virginia, which was about one and a half hours away, for grocery shopping. If we had time, we made a short trip to visit famous places to see new things. With the old Datsun, sometimes Dinh took the whole family to Pittsburgh, New York City, and even Fort Smith to see some of our old friends and relatives.

Despite the fact Dinh and I preferred Vietnamese foods, our children preferred American foods, and they started speaking English at home. To keep up with my children, I started to learn some English for my daily conversation. People from the church were so patient with me. Marian and other ladies took turns driving me to doctor visits. Some days, they took care of Phuong-Anh when my leg was hurting. I felt extremely tired because of my leg combined with my pregnancy. On the weekends, JoAnn and Marian often took us to zoos, farms, and public gardens. Some days, JoAnn did not leave our home until 9:00 PM. The transition to American life would have been much more difficult without the church's help.

I didn't know how to express my gratitude. Two months prior to my baby's birth, on November 13, 1975, JoAnn and other ladies from the church came to pick my family up to visit Mr. and Mrs. Mueller. When I went inside the Mueller's house, many people were there. The ladies of the church had planned a surprise baby shower for me! I was too surprised to say any words. I cried. Perhaps it was the first time in my life that I was so happy I cried. The food was very good too. I tasted fried chicken and pizza for the first time at the party. I've never again had fried chicken as good as that. Since that event, I have learned to like American foods!

In Vietnam, we often did not celebrate the birth of the child until a month after the birth, so I was surprised to receive all kinds of baby gifts from the shower. We took home a car full of gifts. My family had a wonderful time. The food and the gifts were great, but the caring showed by the church members touched us deeply.

# CHAPTER 23

# Mom: Adaptation

Two weeks after we settled down in Maryland, a friend from the church took my husband to a nearby farm. He told Dinh it was time to introduce us to some jobs around the neighborhood. He showed Dinh how to control a lawn tractor and asked if he would like to try.

It was the first time Dinh earned money in America. After four hours of trying to run the tractor, he was offered five dollars cash for his labor. At first, Dinh refused the money, thinking that he was still learning, but the farmer insisted it was Dinh's money and he should keep it. When he got home, he showed me the first five-dollar bill he'd earned. Looking at the money, our eyes filled with tears. We knew there would be much hard work ahead of us to raise a family, soon to be of six children, but we were determined we would make it.

Mr. and Mrs. Verlin Tombaugh were the owners of the house on Harford Road. Two days after Dinh received the money for cutting grass at the farm, Mr. Tombaugh recommended Dinh for a janitor position at Harford Mall, where he could earn $2.10 per hour as a full-time employee. Mr. Tombaugh was a close friend of the Harford Mall's manager at the time. During the first couple of months, before the church gave us the car, Dinh carpooled with several friends from the church. He was punctual and a hard worker, and he got along very well with the janitorial staff. The mall manager, who had immigrated from Hungary, recognized Dinh's hard work and gave him bonuses many times.

I realized how hard it was for Dinh — a teacher and military officer — to work at the mall as a janitor, but because our family needed the income so much, he didn't have a chance to go back to school. Although we appreciated the church's help, we knew we had to be independent, work hard, and keep the family together.

When we first moved out of the Fort Indiantown Gap Refugee Camp, our family received 700 dollars from Church World Services (CWS). This fund was originated from different programs that the United States offered for immigrants. We had placed the fund in our savings in case of emergency. It was time for us to put the fund to good use. We decided to find our own house, whether we rented or bought. We could not depend too much or too long on the hospitality of others.

Pastor Long agreed it was time for us to be independent and have our own place. With the savings we had and with my husband's income, we started searching for a rental house with enough space for eight of us. Pastor Long asked people from the church to help us with the search. Several volunteers took us around their neighborhoods. There was a big house in the suburban area with lots of trees around it. The house probably would be a good size for our family, but I did not want to live there because I was afraid of the loneliness. I imagined days I had to stay at home by myself while Dinh went to work and the children went to school, and I told Dinh that it probably was not a good house for us. Because we didn't have much, we couldn't afford to rent a new house.

Finally, after several unsuccessful times trying to select a suitable house for us, a friend from church agreed to let us rent his property for $100 a month and waived the deposit fee for us. The house was located on Fountain Green in Belair, Maryland. This was an old house made of wood with two stories. There were three bedrooms upstairs. The living room, dining room, and kitchen were located on the first floor. It was a great size house for us, a great beginning in a good location, close to school for the kids and work for Dinh.

On January 14, 1976, our youngest daughter was born. We named her Amy, as a result of our gratitude to the church and a reminder of a universal love from America.

When I was in labor, several church ladies were waiting outside my room at the Johns Hopkins Hospital. They were anxious to congratulate me on the new baby. I felt overwhelmed with their kind hearts and help. They sure treated me as if I was their family.

When Amy was born, her yellow skin made the doctor cautious. Perhaps there were not many Asian people who gave birth at the Johns Hopkins Hospital at the time. Doctors didn't expect babies to have yellow skin; they suspected that Amy might have "yellow fever illness," and to be sure, they wanted to keep her in the hospital for follow-up tests. I was confused to be sent home without my baby at first, but I felt relief after a couple of days, when the tests showed Amy was a very healthy baby. I could take her home to join the rest of her siblings, who were also very anxious to meet the youngest.

After Amy was born, JoAnn and the church staff often visited me and the baby. They gave us lots of winter clothes and baked us lots of cakes and cookies. I remember that when I was in labor, we still lived in the sponsor's house. Ms. Ida Mae told me I had to inform her when I was ready to give birth. With Ida's and the church's help, Dinh was able to take great care of me and the children. When I got home from the hospital with Amy, we moved to the rental house on Fountain Green Road. Again, the church people helped us to move in.

We'll never forget our first rental house. The house was pretty old, and it didn't have an automated heating system. The heater was connected in the back of the house to what I thought was a big tank of gasoline. Perhaps there wasn't much regulation at the time for safety, but the thought of this big gasoline tank exploding made me nervous. After dealing with so many explosions, I became paranoid like my mother-in-law, worrying about the safety of our family.

This was our first winter in America. My children had great fun playing in the snow and building snowmen, but I was freezing and felt the pain inside my leg. Because the house was not insulated very well and because we tried to save money by not burning too much gas, I shivered and felt cold all winter long. After we left Maryland for Arkansas, we learned the house was sold and completely remodeled.

The first winter was difficult for both Dinh and me. On winter days when we had lots of snow, he spent at least an hour shoveling the driveway and clearing the windshield before he could go to work. At first I enjoyed the winter scene, but soon I started to feel miserable — both physically because the cold caused such pain in my body and emotionally because I felt bad Dinh had to work so hard to support us.

My life revolved around my children, especially Phuong-Anh and Amy. Every day, when Dinh went to work and Ngoc, Phuc, Thuy, and Dzung were in school, I stayed at home taking care of my two baby daughters. Two years apart, Phuong-Anh and Amy grew up together, and I believe they were meant to be there for each other. They brightened my day with their talking and their cute faces. They were such good girls when they were young.

Although busy with the girls, I often felt lonely at home. I still missed my mother and other relatives so much, and I found myself isolated from the American society because I couldn't express myself fully. Each time I ate some good food, I wished I could share it with our mothers. Then Tet came, and it reminded me of my past in Vietnam. Even though I didn't say much about my sadness, Dinh recognized the difficulties I went through.

## CHAPTER 24

# Dad: Never Take Things For Granted

I have never taken life for granted. I have taught my children the value of education and hope they understood you have to earn everything in America. I expected my children to help each other be successful in life. At the same time they should never take things for granted. The church members brought food and clothes to my family, but to have the foods and fashions we wanted, we had to work for them.

Although life was not perfect, slowly it changed for the better. I remember when a church member helped us rent our first home. I remember the day I learned to drive and the day I earned my first driver's license. The church taught us to fish rather than fishing for us.

When we gather for good meals on weekends, I sometimes remember when we were very hungry on the Anh Tuan ship. Although the ship had provisions for at least a week, it was overloaded with many people on board. Each family was provided two meals a day, but the portions were not enough.

Phuong-Anh kept crying because of thirst and hunger. She didn't have enough milk to drink for several days on board.

Except for Amy, all our children have experienced hunger. If one has never begged others for a meal, one might not understand what it takes to do so. My family of seven people was given a quart of rice a day. Nga and I dared not eat any because we wanted our five children to have enough. After two days of starving, I begged the cook in the ship's galley to spare us some burned rice at the bottom of the pot. It was hard to swallow this burned rice, but that was all we had.

My mother told me hunger and overwork would make one became unwise. I was unwise when looking at my children suffering hunger. I blamed Nga for forcing me to leave Vietnam, and I was frustrated at having to beg others to eat burned rice from the bottom of the pot. I liked to remind my children to be kind to each other and to never say things that would hurt others' feelings. It is very hard, if not impossible, to take your words back. I felt very guilty for saying the wrong things. When I spoke out of frustration, I made the problems worse, but I did apologize to Nga.

Some people chose to commit suicide when they knew Saigon was lost. Stories about one officer shooting everyone in his family and himself made me regret what I had said to Nga. I learned the hard way to control my emotions. When I was calmer, I knew it was much better to beg for a leftover than to remain in Vietnam and be miserable. It was much better when we had each other. During difficult times, we should share the responsibilities rather than express our frustrations. I learned frustration would not resolve the problems we had. I knew for a fact when people were frustrated, they often made wrong decisions, which could not be described any better than by the Thuong-Tin boat example.

When we were rescued to Guam, we knew a small group of Vietnamese wanted to go back home because they were separated from their families who were left behind. The staff members could not keep the immigrants and sent this group of people back home on a merchant ship, the Viet Nam Thuong Tin. We later learned that the Vietcong ambushed this ship on the Long Tao River with guns and rockets. They killed many passengers on board and captured the rest of the people. All the people on the Viet Nam Thuong Tin who survived were imprisoned for years by the communists.

I believed being patient and having faith would pay off. When we left Vietnam with the Anh Tuan ship, "Nowhere" was our destination. We just hoped to flee the communists, and we hoped to obtain assistance from any overseas friends. Many ships were rescued by Australia, France, and other countries all over the world, but we were among those rescued by America. It was faith that got us rescued by the ship of the American 7th Naval Fleet. Images of the day we were rescued remind me of how well we were treated and how America has helped us build a better future.

## CHAPTER 25

# Dad: My Fondest Memories

The church helped us tremendously. I remember Ms. Ida Mae, a church member who took such great care of us, especially Nga. We stayed with her for several months. Her family lived on the upper floor while we stayed on the first floor. Ida and her family — her sister and two daughters — spent a lot of time and money to help us. She even taught Nga English; she gave Nga a Vietnamese-English dictionary to communicate with her. Ida was very patient and loved us very much.

One day I saw Ida teaching Nga English while warning her to be cautious about snakes when we went camping. Ida wrote the word "snake" on the paper and asked Nga to find that word in the dictionary. Nga has known the word "snake" ever since.

Another great friend was Ms. JoAnn Alderfer, who took Nga to regular doctor visits when she was pregnant. We can't describe how grateful we are to the church people. JoAnn's house was in Baltimore, and to take Nga to a regular visit took her almost an hour of driving, but she always did favors for Nga with a friendly smile. When Mr. James Alderfer took a job in Buffalo, New York, their family moved there and has lived there since. We haven't had a chance to see them yet, but we look forward to that day.

When JoAnn left Maryland, she passed down the assistant's job to Ms. Lois Webb, who was our neighbor for a while. With Ms. Webb's help, Nga adapted to life in America much faster.

Word by word, day by day, we picked up American culture. Life in Maryland wasn't bad, but I felt something was missing. Part of me missed my family, especially my mother, and that made me sad. Although I kept myself upbeat with funny stories, it was difficult to depend so much on others to support my family. The church understood our situation, and they often made special arrangements for us to meet our old friends, such as Lang and Diep, and my relatives.

The church secretly bought two bus tickets for Lang and Diep to visit us. It was on a Saturday, and JoAnn informed us we had a nice surprise awaiting us. All day until after 10:00 PM, we wondered what the surprise would be. We wondered why the church people stayed so late. It was past bed time for our children, almost 11:00 PM.

Then JoAnn appeared at the gate and shouted, "Surprise!" Lang and Diep followed her into the house. JoAnn had gone to the bus station to meet Lang and Diep, who lived in Pittsburgh, Pennsylvania. They had been contacted by the church for a happy surprise visit with our family. We couldn't sleep that night; we had too much catching up to do. The caring of the church people warmed our hearts. We took Lang and Diep to church on Sunday and introduced our long time friends to everyone there.

It was a wonderful blessing to have friends with such beautiful hearts and spirits. We learned that love, respect, and caring are the same in every language. We consider ourselves truly lucky and blessed. All of these people, our friends, will always have a special place in our hearts.

I remember trips to the Oriental markets and picnics the church organized just for our family. It felt great when I could again see other friends we met at the camp. It was amazing how the church loved us unconditionally. We felt they wanted the best for us and respected our Vietnamese tradition of close family relationships.

When we could contact my sister Tran and her family in Arkansas, I knew it was time to say goodbye to Maryland and to become independent. Several days after moving to Arkansas, Nga obtained her first job in the States, and she could help me with extra income to support the family. I landed a better job with better wages. Both our incomes, although modest by American standards, improved our situation considerably.

There were years when we struggled with Nga's leg injury. She endured several surgeries in the States; one of these took her several months to recover. I learned to cook and be the housewife as well as working while Nga was recovering, and I realized how hard it is for women to both hold a job and keep up with the daily chores at home. I learned how challenging it is to be a good cook since I heard my children complaining that my two specialized dishes were not as delicious as their mother's. After six months of taking care of Nga and seeing what she went through, I appreciated what she has given for the Truong-Nhu family.

Even though we've had up and down times in life, after a while, we had saved enough to buy our first home in America. It was a memorable house where we raised all of our children from elementary school through college.

The Vietnamese proverb says, *An cu+, lac nghiep* or "Having a good home is essential to finding a good career." Amy, our youngest child, who was born in America, might not be able to relate to how we grew up. However, I hope she can now understand what this Vietnamese proverb means.

We started our lives in America with a good foundation. Lessons we learned in Maryland and Arkansas and from the church members served us well. From the time we bought our first home in Arkansas, we earned a respectable living, paid our bills and taxes, and usually had money for our children to enjoy. We didn't buy name brand clothing. It was a little hard for our children, who naturally wanted the best, but we learned to budget our incomes. We never wanted our children to have less, but we did make sure they had decent meals and clothes, and most importantly, they could earn their educations and learn the value of money.

## CHAPTER 26

# Mom: Change Again Brings Opportunity

A year after we settled in Maryland, Dinh finally located his sister Tran in Fort Smith, Arkansas. He cheered me up with this good news and let me make the first call to his sister. I was happy to find a relative to talk with. Sister Tran invited us to visit her and her family, and Dinh took some vacation time so we could accept the invitation.

Our children were too excited to sleep the night before we went. Van, a family friend, made the trip with us. I don't know how we managed to fit all nine of us in the old Datsun, even with the two little ones — Phuong-Anh was three and Amy was little more than a year old — but we did it.

The drive from Maryland to Arkansas was more than 1100 miles. We didn't have much money to spend on the trip, and we preferred to eat Vietnamese foods anyway. I cooked rice and salted shrimps and packed lunch bags for everyone, and we stopped to eat at rest areas. We took many pictures along the drive.

Finally, after two days and a night, we reached Arkansas and Sister Tran's house. It had been almost two years since we had seen each other. Greeting us at Tran's house were her daughter and her American son-in-law Bill. Bill had served in the Vietnam War, and we were impressed with his knowledge of the Vietnamese language and culture. During the next days, Tran took us to visit several Vietnamese stores, temples, and restaurants in Fort Smith. Then it was time to go back to Maryland. The visit with Tran warmed my heart. After the trip, I felt less lonely and often called Tran on the weekends to talk.

June 1978. Tran, her husband, her daughter, and son-in-law surprised us with a visit. We were glad to see them but wondered why they were driving such a big truck. We took Tran's family on a tour of Washington, DC.

After a couple of days visiting us, Tran asked, "Would you consider moving south? The weather wouldn't be so hard on your leg. I hate to see you in so much pain from the cold. And all the extra work Dinh has to do shoveling the snow. But most important ... it's good to have family around."

Dinh's brother-in-law told us, "I'll recommend you for a job in Arkansas, working at a food processing company."

Tran added, "If you like the idea, we'll help you move."

Tran's recommendation made a lot of sense. Although we were grateful for all the church had done for us, we believed we needed to take charge of our own lives. I wanted to help Dinh with more income for our family. If we moved south, I would have a chance to work and help support the family.

We rarely made changes without planning, but the opportunity to move south was too good to refuse. After a day of re-thinking the idea, we agreed to the move. We rented a trailer to be hauled by Bill's big truck, said goodbyes to the church members, and headed south to Arkansas.

Our decision surprised our sponsors. They were concerned

it would be difficult for us to make such a big change. Dinh explained to the church that we wanted to be closer to his sister and we also wanted to become independent. After he met with Bill and Tran's family, Pastor Long asked us to keep in close contact with the church, and if needed, let the church know how they could be of any help in the future.

From the day we moved south until now, we have kept in touch with the church and have always thought of the people with much gratitude. We could not have made it without their help, and I am so glad we recently were able to visit some of our family's great friends and sponsors there.

CHAPTER 27

# Mom: New Life in Arkansas

Fort Smith, Arkansas, was a small city. Dinh told me the population was about 70,000 people. The Vietnamese population then was fairly small compared to larger cities on the East and West Coasts. Life would have been more difficult without our relatives' help, especially in the first days. We stayed with Sister Tran for two weeks before we could locate an apartment nearby. The apartment was old, but it had four bedrooms and was close to the schools our children would attend.

Sister Tran helped me obtain a job. With her recommendation, and after a brief interview with the manager, I had my first job in America. I worked at O.K. Foods, Inc., a small food processing company in Arkansas.

The work itself was not hard. Four people sat at a table, cutting chicken into pieces and classifying them into different categories. I had to learn the categories, but after the first few days, it came more easily. The manager assigned me and Tran to sit at the same table, so Tran taught me what she knew. She told me if I liked the job and worked there over a month, she would receive a bonus of $100 for the recommendation.

Every day, I woke up at 5:00 AM and started my day by cooking breakfast for my family. I often cooked lunch for myself and Dinh as well. Because our children were still very young, especially Phuong-Anh and Amy who were not yet in school, Dinh and I had to find jobs on different shifts. He drove me to work at 6:00 AM then came home to take care of the kids. When the older four — Ngoc, Phuc, Thuy, and Dzung — went to school, Dinh took care of Phuong-Anh and Amy, often from 7:30 AM to 3:00 PM.

I came home around 3:00 PM so I could take care of the girls for the rest of the day. If I had to work overtime, Dinh took them to the neighbor, and they stayed there until I came home. I couldn't drive yet, so I often carpooled home with my co-workers. Some days, when I couldn't get a carpool in time, Ngoc got home first, and she took the girls home from the neighbor.

My day usually began at 5:00 AM and ended at midnight. When the kids went to bed around 10:00 PM, I cleaned up the house or did other chores and tried to wait for my husband to come home. Dinh got a job at a warehouse. He had to work overtime as well, and when the warehouse was busy, I didn't get to see him until the weekend.

During the first several years, because I worked hard and often had a perfect attendance record, I earned many bonuses from the company. I made lots of friends from the assembly lines. Several of my younger friends worked during the day and went to school at night. They eventually graduated from college, which I found admirable. To keep the Vietnamese tradition alive in our family, Dinh and I often held outdoor picnics or went fishing with Vietnamese friends.

I remember Fort Smith Park located about forty-five minutes north of the city. We didn't have much but filled our lives with healthy entertainment and outdoor activities. Most of the children loved to be awakened early, sometimes at 5:30

AM, to go fishing at the park. To enrich our lives and keep our eyes open for better opportunities, whenever we were able, Dinh drove the family — me and the six children — to visit other states. We visited Oklahoma, Louisiana, and California where we had relatives and friends who always tried to convince us to move there with them.

Work was difficult, but life was not too bad. We finally saved enough to buy a new car and make a deposit on our first house in Arkansas. We bought the car after the trip to San Diego to visit my cousin Lam. The air conditioning of the old car didn't work while the whole family drove across the desert of Arizona. We were inexperienced in foreseeing the troubles of long distance driving. Thank goodness everyone was still safe after our adventure to California.

The next years became more difficult when many more immigrant workers joined us at O.K. Foods. In contrast with the bonuses I used to receive for having perfect attendance, I could no longer sit down to work. Due to the mass production and output requirements, the assembly lines were modified to produce more. I had to stand to work and had to cut chicken faster to avoid being laid off.

I often wore two or three layers of clothes to protect me from the cold, which was below 32 degrees most of the time. Because of my leg, I couldn't wear the boots that would protect me from the cold water and the temperature. I wore my tennis shoes with double socks, but if the socks got wet, my feet would be numbed.

I asked the managers for support with my injured leg. They were kind enough to locate several chairs along the assembly lines for me but required that I keep up with the speed of the lines. They said if I worked harder, I wouldn't feel the cold as much. I had no choice but to try my best to keep up with the speed of the assembly line because I didn't want to slow others down.

In addition, employees who made mistakes that caused the line to slow down received official warnings from the company. Employees who received three warnings were fired. I started to feel less motivated at work since the stress was very high for me. I didn't like the sound of the alarm clock, and I didn't like the competition at work either. Although I had a difficult time adjusting to the competition, I knew in the long run, it would pay off. During 1983 and 1984, I realized it was very difficult for me to have to carpool all the time, so I decided to learn how to drive. Even with Dinh's help, it still took me twice to pass the driving test. But I finally earned my driver's license and could go to work by myself. Dinh bought me a small Pontiac T1000.

After driving to work by myself for about three months, my car broke down. With the help of some pedestrians, I moved the car into the emergency lane and walked. I couldn't walk fast, and it was late. Fortunately, my neighbor saw me walking and drove me home. After that, my husband and my children told me not to drive anymore. To please them and to keep them from worrying, I didn't drive much. Later when we moved to Dallas, I was intimidated by the big city's traffic and didn't drive anymore.

During 1984, I could see my children growing like weeds. The family's spending kept increasing with different teenager's needs. To make extra income, I applied for a second job, working at night at Tyson Foods, Inc. My health was not so good then because often I had about five hours to sleep every day. I had about one or two hours between jobs from 3:00 to 5:00 PM and didn't get home until 1:00 AM and had to start a new day at 6:00 AM. My body was very tired, but I felt it was worth it to bring home more income to raise my children. I would rather work hard to help my children with their self-esteem. I understood how hard it could be if my children did not have decent meals and clothes.

Dinh saw my health deteriorate from working two jobs. He insisted I had to quit the second job, and he would bring home more income by working more overtime. At first I disagreed, but the cold in the plant made me sick, so I finally quit my second job. We both also agreed it was time to teach our children about the value of education.

The food processing company's business had grown fast. To help families like us, the company offered summer programs for sixteen-year-old teenagers who had parents working with the company. My intention was to teach my children what education could do for them. I didn't want to see them growing up working in the chicken factory all their lives. I discussed with Dinh taking our kids to work at O.K. Foods, Inc. during the summers when they reached the age of sixteen.

I wanted my children to understand that to avoid working in a cold environment like that, they needed to graduate from colleges and find good jobs where intensive manual labor was not a requirement. I wanted them to understand that for us to improve our lives, for none of us to have to wake up at 5:00 AM in the morning, they had to study hard to earn their educations.

In addition, working at O.K. Foods was a good life experience for them. To be accepted, they had to achieve a good academic standard. The summer jobs made them more responsible about studying during school years and gave them some extra cash to spend.

Ngoc and Phuc realized my intentions from the first weeks they worked. Phuc made me promise him that the day he graduated, I would quit my job. He could not stand to see his mom working in the cold for such long hours.

Overall, O.K. Foods was a great opportunity for our family. The company later offered scholarships for employees' children. Thuy, Dzung, and Phuong-Anh all received scholarships from the company, which helped them pay tuition and fees.

I don't regret working for this company. The jokes from my coworkers can still make me laugh. We didn't like Monday very much. The workers often told each other Monday was when we started at the bottom of the hill, Wednesday we were in the middle of the hill, and Friday we had made it to the top of the hill and payday.

1985 was a good year for us. Ngoc received different grants and scholarships to the University of Arkansas in Fayetteville. One of our wishes finally came true when she went to college.

That year was remarkable also because our applications for citizenship were finally accepted. I decided to become an American because I believed Ngoc's future, and my other children's futures, would be bright in this country. My dream has always been to see my children become productive citizens.

## CHAPTER 28

# Mom: America — Our New Home

I call America home. I took my American citizenship test on the fourth of June in 1985, more than ten years after I left my original motherland Vietnam, a month before Independence Day. Perhaps it was the first time I realized the value of independence. I did not take the rights of independence for granted — I earned my American citizenship.

America has taught me to take charge of my life. My husband and I did what we had to do to raise a family of six children. Hard work alone may not be enough to survive. I believe we could not have made it without the low-income assistance in America. During the first few months, the church and the government supported our family tremendously. America was not the golden road many people dreamed of, but it was the land of opportunities for people who worked hard. I am grateful to live in America, to have the chance to build the foundation for my future generations.

Although my husband and I couldn't go back to school, we

felt being full-time parents was paramount to our children. There were hard times when Dinh and I worked long hours, and I often was busy with chores on the weekends. There were happy times when we purchased our first American home. Then all of our children graduated from college.

I call America home. It welcomed us with open arms. However, an adjustment period was necessary.

## CHAPTER 29

# Mom: Dallas: A Destination?

I had promised Phuc when he earned his bachelor's degree, I would quit my job at the chicken factory. I haven't worked since September of 1992, when Phuc joined Ngoc in Dallas and started working as an engineer. Later when Ngoc insisted we move to Dallas with her, Dinh retired and we moved to Texas in June of 1996 to take care of our grandchildren.

Two years after we left Arkansas, my health was much better, but I occasionally felt pain in my ankle. One day, when I took a walk outside the house, I couldn't stand the pain. Dinh took me to Dr. R.W. to see what was wrong.

After a routine x-ray, Dr. R.W advised me to have an operation to connect my ankle joint together with a metal screw. He said the leg had been damaged for so many years it was time for me to do some serious thinking about corrective surgery. At the time I went to Dr. R.W., I had to wear a brace at all times. He said if I followed his instructions, I might not need the brace any longer.

Dallas was a large city compared to Fort Smith, Arkansas, and there were more medical treatment options available there. However, the operation was not as successful as I had hoped. It took Dr. R.W. more than two hours to complete my operation. I had to stay in the hospital for a week, and then I stayed in bed for several months due to complications. Perhaps my body couldn't adapt to the screw technique as it caused me severe pain. After several months in bed, I could participate in a month of physical therapy to practice walking. After a month of physical therapy, I could walk with the help of a brace. My ankle has improved since then, but I still need to wear the brace.

During the time I was again lying in bed in Dallas, Dinh took care of all the chores and cooked for me and the children. For so many times now, he has always been there for me anytime I've needed him. Dinh is my Vietnamese sense of survival. Perhaps the best symbol of Vietnamese tradition for me is my husband Dinh.

CHAPTER 30

# Dad: What America Means

I became more religious when my experiences indicated clearly the circle of life. When we first came to the States, there were several nonprofit organizations asking for donations to support fighting for Vietnam's freedom. When the waves of scandals about misuse of the donated money came to light, we decided to focus on religion to share our beliefs, and we prayed for a brighter Vietnam.

We were blessed to have a better future than the Vietnamese left behind under communism. My sister Giao's husband, who was also a South Vietnamese officer, was sent to the "re-education" camp for thirteen years. She had to raise a family of five children by herself after the communists took everything she had. Her husband returned and her family was sponsored to the States in 1990, when the communist government was trying to normalize relationships with America. Thirteen years in a political prison had made Giao's husband very bitter. From Giao and her family members, we learned more about the hardships suffered by those who stayed in Vietnam after the country fell to communism.

A number of different religions, most commonly Buddhism

and Christianity, were practiced by the Vietnamese community in Arkansas. Although respecting other religions and appreciating the church, we kept our family tradition of following Buddhism. We often gathered with other Vietnamese friends to pray, but in the early days, we didn't have a temple built according to the tradition. The Buddhist population kept growing but we had no formal place to meet, so several local immigrants decided to have a fundraiser to build a pagoda ourselves.

In 1986, The Vietnamese Buddhists of Arkansas Association was formed, and I was selected to be the chairman of the Association. Finally, I could use my knowledge of planning and management to give back to the Vietnamese community. After almost two years of hard work and humble donations, with many hours of labor from many volunteers, a formal pagoda was built in Fort Smith, Arkansas. It was the first for Vietnamese immigrants in the state. When we left Arkansas to move to Texas, I transferred my responsibility for managing the pagoda, which was popular and growing, to other people. When I visit my sister Tran in Arkansas, I often stop by the pagoda. It is satisfying to see I made a worthwhile contribution to the community. For many years, we had wished for a place to release our daily stress, a place where we could spend our valuable time to pray for others, a place we could pray for our mothers and Vietnam. The pagoda was our wish that came true.

America is a melting pot where diversity is valued. America helped us understand where we were coming from and taught us what it means to give back. We learned from the church people about America's generosity and kindness. We learned to make the best out of hardships and to overcome the obstacles in life by working hard. We learned no matter where we came from, America respected our family traditions and provided us a unique opportunity. America may not be perfect, but it is the best country for us.

# CHAPTER 31

# Mom: Vietnam and Me

Living in the United States for over thirty years, I have heard of many bad things that happened to the people who were left behind in Vietnam. Living under communism was very hard for many people.

When the Vietcong invaded Saigon, they arrested all the South Vietnamese officers and forced them to "re-education" camps, another name they used to refer to political prisons. The husband of my sister-in-law was sent to "re-education" camp for over thirteen years; he was tortured and his children were treated unjustly on the outside. Most of his children could not finish school.

Normal civilians had to "donate" many "volunteer" hours, working in the "new economic zone." Communism was taught in K-12 schools, and history was distorted to teach that communism was the best. Kids learned to hate Americans and learned that suicide bombers were heroes. Everyone had to call Ho Chi Minh "uncle," although most people in the South disliked him very much.

In the years of 1975-1979, Vietnamese communists controlled everything in Vietnam. We could not establish direct contact with my mother or my mother-in-law. Because the communists had such closed minds, most families whose relatives were overseas dared not disclose any information. We did not have any word from our relatives in Vietnam until 1977, when we finally heard from my mother-in-law.

During this time, we had to use a third party from France to contact my mother and my mother-in-law. We felt helpless because neither of them was living comfortably. It was sad to imagine how fast our mothers were aging. My mother, although receiving some help from my brothers Anh Hai and Anh Ba, was not happy because she missed all of us.

In 1977, I received a lovely surprise — a letter from my aunt in Silver Springs, Maryland. At the age of eighty, she was one of a million Vietnamese boat people to immigrate to the United States. When I contacted her, I learned more about Vietnam in the first years under the Vietcong.

She told us the Vietcong had taken revenge on people who had any relationship to the South government. Most Vietnamese people didn't have enough to eat. The government controlled everything: how much rice people were allowed to eat, what clothes they could wear, what words they could say, and what lessons they could learn. My aunt knew that to become a boat person was the highest risk that one could imagine. But she said, "I had no choice but to leave Vietnam. I would rather die on the sea than to continue to die slowly under communism."

After days on the sea without destination, my aunt and her daughter were fortunate to be rescued by an American ship which relocated her family to the Songkha Thailand Camp. After two months in the Thailand Camp, she was helped by a committee from the United Nations. Her son TNP and his family lived in Silver Springs. TNP was contacted by the volunteer committee to sponsor my aunt and his sister to the United States. In 1978, we went to visit my aunt. She told me she loved America and thanked Buddha for reuniting her with her children.

During this boat people time, many Vietnamese escaped the communists through trails from Cambodia or Thailand. Corruption happened everywhere. Several relatives who came to the States during the late seventies told me that, not only did they have to leave their properties at home, but after paying the boat or trail owners, they had to bribe the local officers to get by the security gates. There were many cases where people were captured and imprisoned several times until they finally escaped from Vietnam and begged to join the refugee camps sponsored by the United Nations. There was nothing one could lose since the communists controlled everything they had.

Dinh and I sponsored one of our nieces and two other relatives when we found out they stayed at the camp, like we did back in 1975. We learned to expand the circle of life and tried to pay back what we owed to this country by helping others. We treated the sponsored families as we were treated by the church people.

In 1980, when Vietnam's economic crisis arose, with production shortages and extreme dependency on the Soviet Union, boat people continued to escape and die at sea. Then the communists in Vietnam recognized the country needed to be open to foreign economic exchange and technology development, and they finally re-opened the door for foreign investment.

We then could send money and gifts for both our mothers, but our resources were very limited. We had a big family of six children of our own to take care of. In addition, most of the gifts and letters were examined by the Vietnamese government before our mothers received them.

In 1983, we were deeply grieved to receive the news of the death of my mother-in-law. Five years later, my mother died at the age of ninety-four. Both our mothers' wishes to see us one last time went unfulfilled.

Through the Humanitarian Operation (or HO) Program, starting around 1990, we had the opportunity to sponsor two families in the first group of former Vietnamese political and "re-education" camp prisoners admitted to the United States. Later, I learned that my daughter-in-law, Phuong-Thao, and her family came to the States through this program.

Considering all the stories I heard and learned from less fortunate Vietnamese who were left behind, I believe that despite the fact our family went through a lot, we were much luckier. Dinh and I tried our best to help when we were able, to complete the circle of life and set a good example for our children.

## CHAPTER 32

# Mom: Goodbye to My Mother

At the age of twenty-two, I was still very naive — probably too naive to understand all the challenges I would face in life. Being a mother of two innocent kids, my priority was to take care of my family. I didn't care much about politics. I didn't pay any attention to the changes that happened to Vietnam after the Geneva Agreement.

Perhaps I have changed for the better. I have adapted to my new life and learned to pay closer attention to my surroundings. Six months in the hospital and seven years on the run from the communists helped me to value life even more. I left Vietnam to start my new life in America and became an American, but a major part of me still belonged to my mother's land, Vietnam.

I missed Vietnam a great deal, especially when I really focused on the moments alone in the hospitals like many fictional snapshots in time. I reminisced about Hue with much love and sorrow. Many of my loved ones were from Vietnam — some died; some were killed; some were still alive when I left; and some perhaps struggled as much as I had.

I went back to my Vietnam in 1997, after twenty-two

years apart without a single chance to visit my mother. She died without seeing me for the last time. Emotion filled my heart when I remembered the Vietnam of my childhood, the Vietnam of the war years, and the Vietnam of today.

At the time, probably I was very emotional; I couldn't comprehend why my mother decided to stay in Vietnam but approved of my decision to flee to the United States. My mother was torn between me and my brothers as she loved all of us so much. She loved her children equally and unconditionally. Now that I have six children of my own, I understand what she went through.

My mother did love me unconditionally. I remember the days we were on the run from Vietcong, the days we were side-by-side in the pagodas, and the days I was in the hospitals. I remember how my mother held my son Phuc in her arms, how she was willing to sacrifice herself to save him. I remember my mother's sweet voice, trying to comfort me in the middle of the nights, while outside guns fired and mines exploded.

More than several times a day, my mother rubbed my back and told me to close my eyes. She said things would be better after I took a nap, that she would always be right there for me, and that I had nothing to worry about. More than once, when I woke up at night because of the pain from my injured leg, I could feel the warmth of my mother's hands on the front of my head.

Without my mother, I would not have had enough strength to survive. She reminded me of my responsibilities to my kids, and she encouraged me to confront the hardships. I remember a folk song my mother often sang to calm me during the time in the hospitals. I remember the traditional lyrics of the song, which were later rewritten by the musician Y Van,

*Thuong con thao thuc bao dem truong,*
*Con da yen giac me hien vui suong biet bao!*

Or

"Loving you, my child, I don't mind to stay up overnight,.
I really don't mind, as long as you have a good night's
sleep, I am happy!"

For many years, my mother was on the run with us, from
Hue to DaNang and back again to the last time we ran in
1975 from Hue to DaNang to Saigon. I wished my mother
had come with us to the United States, but she decided to stay
in Vietnam after the fall of Saigon with the hope of reuniting
with my brothers, Anh Hai and Anh Ba.

Later when I reestablished the connection with my mother,
I learned that Anh Hai lost his leg during the war. Both Anh
Hai and Anh Ba had married in the North and had many children. Five years ago, Anh Ba died at the age of seventy due to
high blood pressure; he had five children who were still living
in Vietnam though his wife had died earlier in the North due
to illness. I did not have much contact with Anh Hai's and
Anh Ba's families. However, when my mother died, both of
them did pay respect to her and took care of her funeral.

When my mother died, I was in the United States. It was
too far away to be with her or even to see her again for the last
time. I wished I could have told her one more time in person
how much I loved her.

CHAPTER 33

# Mom: Return to Vietnam

In 1997, Dinh and I went back to Vietnam for the first time after twenty-two years far away from my mother's land. It took us a while to plan this trip. When our passport applications were approved, we prepared for the trip with lots of gifts. We brought four huge suitcases; each weighed approximately seventy pounds. My husband and I each had two carry-on bags, the maximum number allowed for international travelers.

Like many other *Viet-Kieus*, a term meaning the Vietnamese who lives overseas, we brought many gifts for relatives and friends. Under the communist society, Vietnamese people loved every single gift brought home from America. After so many years under communism, Vietnamese have become more materialistic because the standard of living is so low in Vietnam.

On the big airplane from Los Angeles to Taiwan, I noticed most people around me were Vietnamese or other Asians. My emotions were in turmoil. I could not believe I could go back and see my mother's land again after all the bad things that happened to us there.

On the airplane from Taiwan to Saigon, I felt excited but also worried. I was excited for the visit, to see some of my loved ones, but I was worried about how the communists would treat us. I could not picture what the Vietcong would be like because all I could remember were the ones I'd met face to face in the Tet Offensive.

We stood in line at Tan Son Nhut Airport. There was a little wall surrounding each customs officer's desk. We noticed differences in the ways people moved through the lines. People whispered in our ears if we paid these officers, they would not cause us any troubles, but if we did not follow the "rule," we probably could not get home to see our relatives in a day.

Seeing others pay the fees, we did the same. There were three or four gates where we presented our paperwork. Each time we passed through a gate, we gave these officers five dollars as a passing fee. The Vietnamese proverb says, *Nhap gia tuy tuc*, or "When you are guest, follow the owner's rules." We definitely did not like the rule of paying fees without receipts, but we had no choice. It was sad. The corruption was obvious, but we could not complain.

My cousins and their sons greeted us at the airport. They lived in Saigon, about a twenty-minute drive from Tan Son Nhut Airport. My relatives took us to their house. I finally had a chance to see Saigon.

Dinh said Saigon had changed a lot. It was even more crowded than during the war, when the Americans came to help the South. Traffic was chaotic with no rules. He told me about five million people lived in Saigon, a population five times what it had been in 1975.

I was scared to see three traffic accidents happen during the twenty-minute drive from the airport to my relatives' house. I saw several police officers in their round hats which reminded me how scared I had been on the run from the communists many years ago ...

During this visit to Vietnam, my husband and I went to see my sister Le and her family in DaNang. She was very old. Time has taken away her strength, and the hard life in Vietnam made her look much older than her years. I wished I had been able to help her sooner, but I was excited to see her and glad to learn she had a happy family.

After receiving news of our Vietnam visit, my husband's relatives came to DaNang to see us. On the trip back to Hue to visit them, we reminisced about the past. I saw many changes from my memories, but this time, the changes were for the better. We passed the Hai Van Hill, now a tourist attraction. *Ao dai*, the traditional long dress, was not as popular as it was before the war. From the way women dressed to the way they talked, I could see they appeared to be more independent.

We visited my mother's old house, which had been occupied by my nephew and his family since my mother's death. I saw the star fruit tree. It was magical that the tree and the fish pond were still there despite all the destruction Hue suffered. My nephew did not have money to repair the house, therefore, all the old holes caused by bullets and rockets' fragments remained, reminding me of the sad times we lived through. The backyard was no longer filled with fruit trees; instead it had been converted into a living area. I gave my nephew some money to repair the house and reminded him to visit my mother's tombstone more often.

We then took a tour around Hue. I remembered both hospitals where I stayed when I was injured. Hue was part of my body. I grew up and went through many up and down times of my life there. My Hue bias made my emotions worse when I visited my old house, where my rice business was built and lost.

As I entered the house, I thought of my mother-in-law. She went back to Hue and stayed in the house when her flight was canceled. She was looking for Minh, the boy we adopted. In a couple of letters exchanged with us in the 80's, my mother-in-law told us Minh came to visit her after a couple of months when everything was controlled by the Vietcong.

When we left Hue, most of the helpers tagged along with our family, but Minh decided to stay. He said he would rather stay there and take care of our family's properties. When my mother-in-law came back, Minh was not in the house. She did not know where he was until one day, wearing a communist officer's uniform, he showed up to see her. My mother-in-law was surprised and thanked Buddha that Minh had not spied on my husband's work while he stayed with us. Perhaps because we treated Minh kindly, he did not set my husband up with a communist arrest nor turn his back to cause us more harm.

Looking at the old house where I lived with my mother-in-law, I reminisced about the history of the house and thought of the faces of many acquaintances. Next to our house was a rental house. The tenants were from different backgrounds, and one of them was an American who had married a Vietnamese woman. The couple often brought us American goods that were considered luxuries during war time ...

I don't know why memories about the American neighbor came back. Perhaps at that moment, as I tried to capture every single detail of the old house and about the neighborhood in Vietnam, I realized the interaction we'd had with all classes of people. We believed whatever we did in life would become a circle later. No matter who we interacted with, we tried to treat them the way we would like to be treated.

Dinh was very happy to see his nieces, the daughters of the pilot, Anh Thung, who died in 1966. There was so much to tell, so much to listen to, and so much to cherish. We were happy to see them grown up and professors at Hue University. They had a happy ending after much sorrow. We were proud of our nieces. They had earned their educations and did not give up.

Our nieces told us when we left Vietnam, they were left behind with my mother-in-law, and they had a tough time fighting for their educations. Because my brother-in-law was a South Vietnamese officer, they were discriminated against by the local governments. Our nieces were classified as *Con cua My Nguy*, or Children of Untruth Vietnamese and American. They told us they were forced to live in the "new economic zones" where they did not have enough to eat for years. It was hard for them to survive, but, thank Buddha, they did make it.

We then made a trip to Dau Giay, a small town located about sixty kilometers east of Saigon. We reunited with brother Tho's wife. Unable to escape from Vietnam after 1975, Tho's family was forced to Dau Giay, a "new economic zone." With Tho's death during the war, his wife had to work to support a family of four children. The first and the third daughters became boat people during the eighties. Tho's wife is now living in Vietnam with the help of her daughters in America. Tho's second child, a son, and the youngest daughter still live in Vietnam with his wife. They have survived great difficulties, and with the help of the two daughters in Arkansas, their lives are getting better.

Two of our main purposes for visiting Vietnam were to visit our mothers' tombstones and to repair our mothers' old houses in Hue. With my children's help, we took some money to Vietnam that could be used to remodel our parents' tombs. After the remodeling was done, we rented a big van to invite all the relatives to come celebrate the remembrance for our parents.

Three weeks in Vietnam went by pretty fast. I was glad we could go back for a visit. In the future, if conditions allow, I hope I can return one more time. The next time I would like to take my children with us. I wish I could travel from the North to the South of Vietnam, to learn more about my mother's land and appreciate more where I came from.

I came back to the United States with a sense of satisfaction and a more peaceful mind. It was nice to visit my mother's land, but we were excited to come to back to America ... back to our home.

CHAPTER 34

# Mom: Hope —
# Past and Future

I didn't mind working hard. It has been rewarding to see each of my children become successful in life. The old Vietnamese proverb *Con hon cha, nha co phuc* or "If your children have a better life than yours, your family has been blessed" describes my situation. My heart overflows with gratitude to Buddha. I appreciate the beautiful family he has given me and the companionship Dinh and I have shared.

We both agreed hope held our family together. Our hopes were born with our children. Like candle flames, sometimes they flared, and then subsided, until the winds of war almost extinguished them. We treasured our hopes and shielded the tiny flames on the long journey from our native land to America and through the challenges of raising our family.

Our hope was realized, our first wish came true, when Ngoc earned her degree. Then, each of our children graduated from college. The results of thirty-five years of hard-work and high hopes — an American dream came true.

Growing up in America, my children don't remember or understand much about Vietnam. Amy was born in Maryland, so Vietnam is a foreign country to her. I would like to preserve the past and connect to the future by teaching my children, especially the young ones, about the Vietnamese language and culture.

CHAPTER 35

# Mom: Our Children Today

During the time Ngoc studied at the University of Arkansas, I missed her deeply because she was the first to leave home. Dinh drove the kids and me to visit her at the University almost every weekend. I questioned the quality of the meals she ate in school and cooked Vietnamese dishes and dried goodies for her.

Ngoc was studious and set a great example for her younger siblings. She graduated with a bachelor's degree in 1989 and earned her master's degree in 1990. The following year, she married Thanh, who she'd met in her sophomore year. Although we were sad to see them move to Dallas, we were happy she had her first job there. And we knew Thanh would take good care of our daughter.

Of all my children, Phuc most reminds me of the past in Vietnam because we were injured together during Tet of 1968. He was a good boy and showed his love liberally with lots of hugging and kissing. I often joked that the girls would run away if he kept kissing me and teasing so much. When he was young, Phuc was quite a playful character. Outgoing, with a great sense of humor, he wasn't afraid to show his emotions.

He enjoyed spending time with Amy and Phuong-Anh and helped them with school and sports. Perhaps Phuc was born to be in America — his personality is very American. Independent, with a strong will, he easily adapted to the new culture.

Although Phuc was not as studious as Ngoc, he was very determined to graduate, especially after he worked summers at OK Foods. It broke his heart to see me working in the cold temperature. At that young age, he realized the value of education and the difference an education would make to the family. Phuc made me promise I would quit working in the chicken factory when he earned his bachelor's degree and found his first job. I thought it would be a good motivation for Phuc to study harder, so I agreed.

When Ngoc was a sophomore, Phuc joined her at the University of Arkansas. He majored in electrical engineering and graduated in May of 1991. After graduation, he joined Ngoc in Dallas and found his first job. He also went to graduate school to earn a master's degree in telecommunications. With Ngoc's and Phuc's financial support, Dinh agreed it was time for me to retire. I kept my promise to them and retired in July of 1991, two months after Phuc earned his bachelor's degree and landed a job. After almost fifteen years working in the food processing industry, I retired to stay home and take care of the house.

Ngoc and Thanh had their first baby, Ailien, in 1991, the same year Phuc graduated. In 1996, after Ngoc gave birth to Caitlin, Dinh and I moved to Dallas to help her with her new baby. By this time, Thuy and Dzung had also settled in Dallas. We arranged for housing, tuition, and other fees to support Phuong-Anh and Amy in their college educations prior to our move. Ngoc, Phuc, Thuy, and Dzung all helped us support their younger sisters. Ngoc and Thanh had their first son, Ty, in 1998.

My husband and I always wanted to tell our life story to our children and grandchildren. We want our future generations to learn and remember our family history. Phuc married in 2003, a year before this book was started. Phuc's wife, Phuong-Thao, was an ideal addition to the Truong-Nhu family as she was the perfect family member to translate the family story. Phuong-Thao grew up in Vietnam and worked as a professional in both cultures. Hence, she was fluent in Vietnamese and English. Phuong-Thao and Phuc have worked very hard to translate our memoirs, which were written in Vietnamese.

Thuy was born in 1970, during one of the most emotional times of my life. Perhaps she inherited her emotional character from me because of the experiences I suffered. When Thuy was little, she was a very girly girl. During her years in high school, she participated in beauty contests and once finished in the top five. Only five years old when we came to the United States, she was too young to remember much about Vietnam though she did make an effort to keep the language.

Introverted and studious, Dzung was four years younger than Phuc. Dzung enjoyed electronics, reading, and playing with Amy and Phuong-Anh. He also showed his love with hugs. Both of our sons accepted responsibility early. When Ngoc and Thuy got married, Dzung and Phuc helped to support their younger sisters until they finished college.

A couple of years after Phuc went to college in Fayetteville, Thuy and Dzung followed him, also majoring in electrical engineering. They both received their degrees in 1994 and joined Ngoc and Phuc in Dallas. Thuy worked for Ericsson while Dzung's first position was with Compaq.

Dzung married in 2002 to Vu-Thy, a traditional Vietnamese who was originally from Hue. Vu-Thy reminded me of my youth in Hue. Dzung was very lucky to meet her, especially since Vietnam has been through so many changes, causing people to lose sight of traditional values for materialism. In this modern world, the Vietnamese traditional values Vu-Thy brought to the Truong-Nhu family are very precious. In December 2005, Dzung and Vu-Thy had their first child, a son they named Nicholas.

Thuy met her husband Douglas while working at Ericsson. They have two beautiful girls, McKenzie and Kennedi, who remind me of Thuy when she was little. McKenzie, who turned seven in November of 2005, is articulate and caring with her family and grandparents. She understands Vietnamese fairly well although she cannot yet speak the language.

In 1986 Phuong-Anh, who was as determined as Phuc, asked to join the cheerleading team at her middle school. We tried to explain we didn't want her to try out for cheerleader because we were concerned we could not afford her expenses. In addition, Dinh's working schedule and only one car would make it difficult for us to take her to practice and camps.

To become a cheerleader, Phuong-Anh had to compete against twenty other girls. In addition to our concerns about money and transportation, we were also worried that the cheerleading activities would distract her from studying. However, we agreed to allow her to try out. When Dinh took her to the competitions, I hoped she would not be selected. But — to our surprise — Phuong-Anh was chosen. Not only was she selected, but also she became very popular at her high school.

With peer pressure, Phuong-Anh wanted to have all the luxury accessories a normal cheerleader would have, and she developed an increased taste for clothes, shoes, and make-up. During her three years in high school, both Dinh and I invested a great deal of time and money on her activities to keep her on track with studying. I remember every year, each time she tried out, we hoped she wouldn't be selected so she could concentrate more on studying. Ironically, Phuong-Anh was always selected.

Amy also joined the cheerleading team at her high school. The expenses for Phuong-Anh's and Amy's cheerleader activities got worse. To raise money to pay, I took the cheerleading products such as cookies or candies to sell to my co-workers who honestly couldn't afford them, but who bought them with a smile. I spent a lot of my lunch and break time selling for my girls. With our humble incomes, we struggled to make enough for the monthly bills. I tried without success to find a second job to help Dinh with extra expenses.

In April 1983, my leg throbbed and ached at work one day. During break, I looked and saw a red circle around the knee. I called Dinh to take me home and then asked my supervisor for a day off. My husband took me to the emergency room, where they told me I had a slight fever.

A doctor at the hospital told Dinh I had an infection from my old injury. I don't remember the doctor's name, but I remember one of his legs was shorter than the other and he walked slowly. He added that the tiny rocket fragments left in my leg had become infected and were causing the pain. He prescribed an antibiotic to cure the infection and ordered me to take at least three weeks off from work.

Before returning to work, I took the doctor's note to my employer to arrange for a special seat at my work station. Due to my injured leg, I could no longer stand on the assembly line like my coworkers. My supervisor gave me special preferences and allowed me a lighter work load.

Phuong-Anh realized college was fast approaching, and she studied hard so she wouldn't disappoint us. Her hard work earned her an annual O.K. Foods scholarship that is awarded to only one employee's son or daughter each year.

A month later, my health had not improved. Dinh worked overtime, but it was still difficult to make ends meet. Every Saturday, he was among the first to volunteer to work overtime. We wanted our children to focus on school and not worry about our finances. We just didn't want them to know our situation because it might affect their self-esteem. We wanted them to have the same opportunities others enjoyed. We wanted to give our children the unconditional love our mothers had given us. Amy and Phuong-Anh participated in many extracurricular activities. They didn't realize what a sacrifice it was for us to pay their cheerleading expenses. However, we didn't mind working hard for the opportunity to see our girls shine.

Amy was luckier than Phuong-Anh because the last years she was in high-school, Ngoc and Phuc had already started working in Dallas, and our financial status had improved.

During her senior year, Amy was elected Senior-Maid for the Football Homecoming Court. It was an exciting time for her, and she wanted a special dress for the momentous occasion. Although Dinh and I wanted to buy her a nice dress, the one she selected was too expensive. We couldn't tell her "no," so we bought the dress. Homecoming day was important to her.

We started out watching Amy during the pep rally and then followed her downtown where she rode in the parade. She looked beautiful that night as Dinh escorted her onto the field with the entire family watching, just as we did for most of Phuong-Anh and Amy's games. Memories of our children's shining moments will always be with us, and naturally, the parents' pride makes our lives complete.

Phuong-Anh and Amy were the continuation of our hopes coming true. Both girls were privileged to have support from their siblings. In return, we knew they appreciated where they came from and worked hard to earn their educations. Both graduated from college. Phuong-Anh majored in education, and Amy majored in biology, and both have successful careers.

Phuong-Anh is now a mature and responsible woman. She married Bryan Gist, and they had their first baby Emma in

2005. Amy married Rob Craig and had their first baby, a girl named Natalie, in December 2005. Phuong-Anh and Amy have always been close. Even though they are far away from us, we are happy they live close to each other in Lowell, Arkansas.

Dinh and I are so blessed to have such a wonderful family: six children, four sons-in-law, two daughters-in-law, and eight grandchildren ... so far. We are all healthy and happy. Our family continues to grow. In addition to the wonderful grand-daughters and grandsons already here, there are more on the way. We cannot wait to meet the newest members of our family and share with them the love we have.

Personally, I love all of them very much, and know, in return, they also love us very much. During the holidays, our big family gathers together and enjoys traditional Vietnamese meals. Our hopes have come true — an American dream has come true for Dinh and me.

CHAPTER 36

# Dad: The Journey Back

In February 2005, our oldest daughter Ngoc informed us she was going to attend a conference in Baltimore in June. She excitedly asked if we were interested in making the journey to visit old friends. My wife and I didn't think twice. We readily accepted the invitation to make this trip.

Soon after, Ngoc called Mr. and Mrs. Norman Bollinger, who were part of the church family who helped us tremendously in 1975. They were ecstatic to hear about our visit and couldn't wait for the day. We, too, could hardly contain our excitement. We happily made plans over the phone for those precious days in June.

As we made our way through the winding country roads of suburban Baltimore, fond memories flowed freely. The lush vegetation and scenic views were welcoming sights, so different from our current home, Dallas. The green, rolling hills and white picket fences were picturesque, and the fresh morning air was brisk and refreshing. The thick forest lining the countryside provided a majestic backdrop as we traveled the forty minutes or so to our destination.

We drove to the house that we called home our first couple

of months in the States. Staring at the Harford house, we marveled at how little it had changed. The black shutters, the stately trees, and well-manicured lawns looked as they had nearly thirty years ago. Nga, Ngoc, and I savored this moment for a few more minutes and then moved on to our next destination. The area definitely was more commercially developed. Surprisingly, my sense of direction was fine, as if some force directed us where to go.

Our next visit was Harford Mall, my first place of employment after coming to the States. I had fond memories of this special place that had been a part of my life for three years. After taking snapshots for keepsakes, we headed to Norman and Marian's.

The drive was longer than I remembered, but we eventually reached the home where they had hosted a couple of unforgettable birthday parties for our children. Marian was sitting outside awaiting our arrival. We quickly made our way out of the vehicle and toward the house, where we firmly hugged our dear friend. Over a homemade dinner, we caught up with each other's families and reminisced about many memorable moments of those past years. One priceless moment that made its way into our conversation was the "sugar/cigar" incident.

It was in the summer of 1975. We had just barely settled in the Harford Road home. Marian hustled all seven of us (Amy had not been born yet) into her compact Datsun. To this day, we don't know how all of us including Norman and Marian's two little ones were able to squeeze into that little car.

It was doubtful anyone had a seatbelt on. Unlike today, seatbelts simply weren't emphasized during those years. While Norman was at work, Marian was kind enough to take all of us to the local grocery, a Safeway. Looking back, we must have been quite a sight to shoppers in the store that day — two Asians with five flustered little ones, all about one year apart, and three Anglos winding their way through aisle after aisle. My wife Nga was specifically looking for sugar. Suffice it to say, our English at the time was poor. My foreign language was French, and I had learned some English, just enough to make sense with American advisors. Perhaps I'd never used the word "sugar" before in conversation with Americans. When I mentioned in my thick accent to Marian that we needed "sugar," the pronunciation came out as "cigar."

Marian was immediately taken aback by this request. After all, her and her husband's faith and belief strictly prohibited any smoking or alcohol. To make things worse, her little boy, Jonathan, blurted out, "I'm telling Daddy!"

Marian quietly and quickly interjected, "Jonathan, shut up, just shut up!" Nevertheless, she guided our large group to the cigarette aisle. Once again, Jonathan started threatening, "Daddy will be mad when he finds out!" Marian patiently shushed Jonathan. "Be quiet; please, be quiet!"

Startled at the sight of these products, Nga quickly shook her head to express disapproval and non-interest.

Marian, at this point, was thoroughly confused, asking, "Do you want the thick ones, thin ones, long ones, or short ones?"

Nga continued to shake her head and in despair walked away. We all followed suit. Then, as Nga entered a random aisle on our way out, she walked past some small, carefully stacked packages. One package had a tiny hole in it. Hence, grains of sugar had trickled from the package. Nga took her fingers and dabbed the tiny grains. With barely contained excitement and a huge grin, she looked at Marian.

At this point, Marian finally understood and exclaimed, "You want sugar!"

Later when I told this incident to Norman, I told him I should write the word "sugar" on paper to avoid confusion.

During our reminiscing, Marian reminded us about the

part of the story where she told her son to "shut up!"

We all exploded in laughter. Before we knew it, it was 10:30 PM, and we were totally exhausted with lots of memories.

### ###

It was a clear, mild morning, and we were eating breakfast before heading to the Long Green Valley Church for services. Before leaving, Marian updated us on the lives of some of our other church friends. We were excited about seeing so many friends in one place.

The church hadn't changed at all. Other than an addition to the back of the building, everything remained the same. The church had an elderly, yet dignified and graceful, feel to it. We immediately felt at home. Marian took us on a quick tour and pointed out some current projects she was working on. After touring and catching up with other friends, we took our seats for the morning service. Once the service concluded, we continued catching up with other folks whom we hadn't had a chance to say "hello" to. Marian had planned an open house for anyone interested in stopping by her house for a light lunch and refreshments. She murmured reminders to several people, and we were on our way.

### ###

The room was as I remembered nearly thirty years ago. It was simply adorned, nothing too fancy, but I recall it being one of the most comfortable, inviting rooms we'd ever seen. My heart was filled to bursting — the room was brimming with cheerful smiles and soft chatter. No other room could have been filled with more warmth or love than that room was now. The table in the corner was adorned with festive party items and scrumptious food and flanked by vivid balloons. Gentle music filled the air.

I turned to one of my friends, whom I had not seen in nearly thirty years, and thought how blessed my family was to have known all these wonderful people. They had shown a genuine kindness that astonished and touched me as deeply today as it had all those years ago. She murmured something, but I'm not sure what her words were. I was content in the moment, savoring the precious time spent with friends whom we had not seen in so long.

Flashbacks came to me — memories of the days when these strangers threw birthday parties (one or two in this same room) for our children, a simple act that touched us deeply and made them feel so special, knowing someone cared about them. The images faded, and I snapped back to the present — friends mingling with one another and catching up on news. A strong nostalgic feeling overcame me.

When the party was in full swing, we found out it was also to celebrate Ngoc's thirty-ninth birthday. It was so touching that Marian and our other friends remembered the date. Ngoc was deeply touched too. She opened each and every birthday card containing good wishes from everyone. It was deja vu all over again. This party was just like those many years ago when Marian and other ladies took turns hosting birthday parties for our children and a surprise baby shower for Nga. Those thoughtful gestures by these gracious and kind women had eased our transition into our new home.

We were mingling, updating one another about our families and careers, and just enjoying the company. We savored the treats Marian and the other ladies had made and then capped the party off with homemade ice cream and cake.

Before heading back to Dallas, we had one last surprise waiting for us. A church couple, Charlie and Edna Mueller, who hadn't been able to make it to the get-together, came to see us. We expressed our delight and hugged them both tightly. We had a lovely dinner and then sadly said our goodbyes.

Charlie and Edna invited us to visit their home after that. Their house on Harford Road bought back many memories of thirty years ago — a baby shower for Nga and several birthday parties for Phuc, Dzung, and Thuy. The house had been remodeled to more modern architecture, but the feeling of hospitality remained. In a large living area, the Muellers had placed their collection of dolls. The living room reminded Nga of how kind the Muellers had been to us. We took many pictures, pictures that took us back to the good old days. Deep down, we hope it won't be another thirty years for the next reunion.

CHAPTER 37

# Mom: Appreciation

America brought me independence and freedom. I thank America for making my life so bright. America helped strengthen our family values. Freedom has eased the pain I felt during the Vietnam War. My children have better lives in America. Freedom and independence are priceless.

Dinh and my children have brought me happiness. Without Dinh, I don't know where I would be today. I thank him for always being there for me. Because of all the things — good and bad — we've shared, he is first in my heart. Thank you, Dinh, my dearest love. I love you even more than the day we married.

To my children, my children-in-law, and my grandchildren: I love each of you the same. I hope you love each other and care for your children the way we have loved and cared for you. Always remember the endless love of your grandmothers that enabled me to survive and care for you after I became partially disabled as a young woman. I hope you cherish the memories and pay respect to your ancestors, especially your grandparents. I am proud of each of you and hope you will keep the family history alive and maintain the family tradition.

## CHAPTER 38

# Dad: Friendships and Family

During our first days in the States, my family had to adjust to new faces, culture, and language, but I knew deep down this great country offered something that Vietnam could not, and that was freedom. In addition, this grand country helped us maintain wonderful friendships over the years and become better people ourselves.

Among the kindhearted people we should thank are our sponsor families at the church and Pastor and Mrs. Long. We stayed at the Tombaughs' home for the first few months. Each church family volunteered their time and money to help us with the adjustment. The Muellers spent time with my children almost every day and took care of Nga when she was pregnant. The Tombaughs taught my children English and took them out to play with their children, while the Bollingers often took my family to the City Zoo and Arboretum where we learned many new things about American culture and had great times. I felt no barriers even though our languages were different — these caring church members made us feel at home. We would not be where we are today if the church, especially Pastor Long and the Alderfers, hadn't helped us. When the Alderfers moved to New York, Ms. Lois Webb often came to visit and helped when we needed her.

Every one of us changed throughout the years, even traditional Nga. She learned to feel more comfortable when church members and her coworkers, particularly men, hugged her. It was not our custom for different genders to hug each other, but Nga adjusted to the new affections because she became an American herself. She did not like American food, but she learned to cook many different American dishes. She couldn't picture herself working in an American factory, but she did it. America created the opportunities for us to start again. In spite of the difficulties, we took the opportunities and made the most of them.

Because I had six small children, I couldn't attend college in the United States. I had to work to support my family. I started as a custodian which, honestly, embarrassed me. The Vietnamese culture bias caused me to have low self-esteem and a prejudiced attitude. I was a proud man and knew I had to earn for our future, but working as a custodian actually drained my motivation. I was once a teacher and an officer, and such a huge change proved to be very challenging for me. I learned to adapt to the system, and I learned that, no matter where I started, if I worked hard to prove myself, life for the family would be rewarding in the future.

One thing I learned was that, no matter where you go, without education, you won't have as many options as you wish. I didn't have a chance to go back to school, but I did what I could to keep my family together. I was willing to have less, but I dreamed of my children going to college because it was the only way we could get out of the cycle of poverty. I learned Vietnamese tradition and American culture were actually in agreement about the need for a better education.

Education taught me never to settle for less, and I didn't. I asked my children to have better educations and better careers than I had, and I took the opportunities America gave me to do the best I could for my children.

I was lucky to have such a loving family. All of my children make me proud, and Nga has been a wonderful partner. The only thing I regret is I didn't make enough money to support my mother who I left behind in Vietnam. I wish I could have helped her sooner and that I could have gone back to see her for one last time. By the time I had a better job and started saving more and my family had better clothes to wear and better meals to eat, my mother had already passed away.

I appreciate life although it wasn't easy for my family. I learned to be optimistic because we now have our freedom and live in America. We never forget what America has done for us and how it accepted us with open arms. Life in America hasn't been easy, but we've learned that with persistence and determination, we will achieve our goals.

If we can't accomplish everything during our life time, we hope that our future generations will. Both Nga and I hope our children will remember family is the foundation for everything they do in life. Family is the basis of society, keeping everyone together no matter how hard the situation becomes. With family support, one can survive all obstacles, build from the beginning, and make a positive impact on society.

Nga often reminded our children how hard it would be for us without the family foundation. When she was injured, she was very young and sometimes felt depressed about her partially disabled leg. For years living in Vietnam, with my support, Nga overcame her low self-esteem to become a strong-willed woman. In return, for years living in the United States, Nga supported me with so many roles, both socially and within the family.

Nga told my children about her learning experience, a treasure life has given her. She often reminds us how much money we saved by having her as the family "barber." For over thirty years in the States, she has always given me a hair cut when I need it. She told our girls her cooking skills are improving almost every day, from the time when she didn't know any dishes and was spoiled by her mother, to now when she can cook almost every single famous dish of Hue. She can also sew some basic clothing. She told our children living on a humble income forces people to be more creative and enhances their adaptation skills. Nga is a great example of a Vietnamese woman who is traditional and supportive of family. I thank Buddha, who has granted me a beautiful family, especially an admirable and loving wife.

CHAPTER 39

# Dad: Retirement and Hopes

I retired in 1996 when we moved to Dallas. I retired early so I could be with my children who plan to stay in the Dallas area. My family has grown from eight of us to a large extended family of twenty-two people (at this writing) with more to come: Ngoc and Thanh, who have three beautiful children, Ailien, Caitlin, and Ty; Phuc (or Kenny) and Phuong-Thao (or PT), who were the last in the family to marry; Thuy and Doug, who have two adorable girls, McKenzie and Kennedi; Dzung and Vu-Thy, who have a baby son Nicholas; Phuong-Anh and Bryan, who have a cute little girl named Emma; and finally Amy and Rob, who have a new baby daughter Natalie. The first four couples — Ngoc and Thanh, Kenny and PT, Thuy and Doug, Dzung and Vu-Thy — live close to us. The last two couples — Phuong-Anh and Bryan, and Amy and Rob — still live in Arkansas.

Many Sundays, we gather at my home so we can share family time and eat Vietnamese traditional foods for dinner. Every occasion, the extended shopping list keeps getting longer and longer for us! Nga and I are happy to see that our children and grandchildren are so close to each other, and we are glad we created the family tradition of gathering. In this modern world, family closeness is a treasure for us!

It is an American dream come true. From a "white hand" with nothing and with six children, we are now a big extended American family. We have learned life's valuable lessons, and we appreciate America for giving us the opportunities. We believe in hard work and optimism. We believe in the idealism of planning and setting goals in life. Now that our six children already have their own families, like a Vietnamese poet says, *Thanh thoi tho tui ruou bau,* or "Relax and have some wine" — we are ready for our time of doing what we like.

Our youngest daughter Amy is very Americanized, but we are glad that she can still keep the family tradition alive. Although she grew up with mostly American friends and can't write or read Vietnamese, Amy can still communicate and talk with us in our mother language. Amy is the *ut* or the youngest so we sometimes give her special attention.

Nga often joked with Amy that, among the six children she had, Amy was the only one who didn't cause labor pains during delivery. In Vietnam, the medication wasn't so modern, and labor could last days. Nga told Amy with advanced medicine, it was easy to give birth to the *ut*. We were lucky to arrive in America, where the standard of living is higher than Vietnam.

Amy grown up is our hope grown up. Her birth marked the end of the saddest period and the beginning of a brighter time for the Truong-Nhu family. She often asks me and Nga about Vietnam and our family history. Her curiosity was the motivation for this book. We hope when Amy, Phuong-Anh, and everyone in our extended family read these memoirs, they will appreciate the Vietnamese culture. I hope they will keep the Vietnamese-American tradition alive. We hope our future generations will learn to appreciate both the American and Vietnamese cultures that will enable them to be successful.

We speak for most Vietnamese Americans when we say we are appreciative for everything the Americans have done for us, especially the soldiers and their families for making the ultimate sacrifices. We owe this country our gratitude and know it will be impossible to repay America. We will do our part to be productive citizens and to promote the value of Freedom.

*Appendix 1*

# Sir Truong-Nhu Cuong Eulogy

Excellences, Messieurs,

C'est avec une émotion profonde et une grande tristesse que je viens, au nom du Gouvernement français, saluer d'un adieu suprême et respectueux la dépouille mortelle de S. E. Truong-Nhu-Cuong.

L'exposé sommaire de la carrière de cet éminent mandarin est le plus grand éloge qu'on puisse faire de ses hautes qualités de savoir et d'intelligence.

Né en 1843, S. E. Truong conquit le titre de Cu-Nhon au concours triennal de 1867, c'est-à-dire à l'âge de 24 ans. Il débuta dans le mandarinat en 1871, et franchit rapidement les grades supérieurs.

En 1885, il était déjà Phu-Doan de la province de Thua-Thien En 1886 et 1887, il dirigeait la province de Thanh-Hoa en qualité de Tong-Doc Il fit preuve dans ces fonctions, particulièrement difficiles à cette époque de rébellion, d'une énergie, d'une activité et d'une savoir faire qui lui conquirent la sympathie et l'admiration de tous les officiers et fonctionnaires français.

Peu après, en 1888, il fut appelé à Hué et chargé par intérim du Ministère des Finances.

Depuis lors, et jusqu'au jour de sa retraite, c'est-à-dire pendant 29 ans, il ne quitta pas la capitale.

Il assura successivement la direction du Ministère des Finances, du Ministère de la Guerre, du Ministère des Travaux Publics et enfin du Ministère de l'Intérieur.

Enfin, depuis 1906, il assuma la présidence du Conseil des Ministres.

Pendant la même période, il fut chaque année désigné comme membre titulaire du Conseil Supérieur de l'Indochine.

Entre temps, il recevait du Gouvernement français la Croix de Commandeur de la Légion d'Honneur en 1913, tandis que le Gouvernement annamite lui décernait successivement les grades de Vo Hien et de Van-Minh, et les titres de noblesse de Hien-Luong Ba et Hien-Luong Hau

Telle fut la remarquable carrière administrative et politique de S. E. Truong-Nhu-Cuong qui, pendant plus de quarante années, exerça des fonctions d'autorité, et pendant trente ans participa comme ministre, avec une activité sans cesse en éveil et un inlassable dévouement, au gouvernement du peuple annamite.

Le Gouvernement annamite et le Gouvernement français perdent en S. E. Truong un serviteur fidèle. Personnellement, je ne saurais oublier que pendant quatre années ce grand mandarin n'a cessé de m'aider de sa collaboration sincère et éclairée. Et je n'oublierai pas non plus que tout récemment encore, alors que son grand âge l'avait depuis bientôt deux ans obligé à quitter le pouvoir, l'ancien Président du Co-Mat tint à venir personnellement, après la signature de l'armistice, m'exprimer la joie qu'il avait ressentie en apprenant la grande victoire française.

Voilà pourquoi je disais tout à l'heure combien il m'était douloureux de voir disparaître dans la tombe la dépouille mortelle de S. E. Truong-Nhu-Cuong que j'espérais voir jouir longtemps encore d'une retraite si bien méritée.

Au nom de tous les Français, je souhaite que le repos éternel lui soit léger ; je donne à ses amis, à ses collègues et à tous ses compatriotes l'assurance que son souvenir restera gravé dans nos mémoires comme celui d'un loyal ami de la France.

E. Charles

•  •  •

Your excellencies, Ladies and Gentlemen,

It is with deep emotion and great sadness that I have come to offer my last and respectful salute to the remains of S.E. Truong-Nhu-Cuong in the name of the French Government.

A simple exposition of the career of this eminent Mandarin constitutes the best eulogy which could be given to his superior endowments of knowledge and intelligence.

Born in 1843, S. E. Truong earned the title of "Cu-Nhon" at the tri-annual contest in 1867, at the age of 24. He made his entry into the Mandarinate in 1871, and gained quick access to the highest ranks.

In 1885, he was already the "Phu-Doan" of the Thua-Thien province. In 1886 and 1887, he led the Thanh-hoa province in the "Tong-Doc" capacity. He carried out his duties in this particularly difficult period of rebellion, demonstrating a level of energy, initiative and skill which earned him the sympathy and the admiration of all the French officials.

Shortly thereafter, in 1888, he was called to Hue and installed as interim Finance Minister. Since that time, until the time of his retirement twenty-nine years later, he never left the capital. Since that time, he held the positions of Finance Minister, War Minister, Public Works Minister, and finally Interior Minister. Finally, since 1906, he took on the responsibility of President of the Ministerial council.

During this same period, he has been designated, each year, as a titular member of the Superior Council of Indochina. In the meantime, he received the Commander's Cross of the Legion of Honor from the French Government in 1913, while the Annamite Government awarded him the ranks of Vo-Hien and Van-Minh, and the Nobility titles of Hien-Luong-Ba and Hien-Luong-Hau.

Such has been the remarkable administrative and political career of S. E. Truong-Nhu-Cuong, who for more than forty years exercised authoritative functions, and for thirty years participated in the government of the Annamite people at the ministerial level, showing an unfailing dedication to the Annamite people and its government.

The French Government and the Annamite Government lose a faithful servant in the distinguished person of S. E. Truong. Personally, I will never forget that for forty years this great Mandarin has never failed to grant me the benefit of his sincere and lucid collaboration. I will never forget either, that recently, as his advanced aged had forced him to relinquish power some two years ago, the former president of the Co-mat made a point of visiting me personally, following the signature of the armistice, to express the joy he had felt when learning of the great French victory.

This is why I felt such distress when seeing the remains of S. E. Truong-Nhu-Cuong being deposed in their resting place. I had hoped to see him enjoy for many more years the pleasures of such a well deserved retirement. In the name of the French people, I wish him a peaceful eternal repose. I assure all his friends, colleagues and compatriots that he will forever be engraved in our memory as a faithful friend of France.

E. Charles